THEOLOGIANS TODAY: EDWARD SCHILLEBEECKX

THEOLOGIANS TODAY: a series selected and edited
by Martin Redfern

EDWARD
SCHILLEBEECKX
OP

SHEED AND WARD · LONDON AND NEW YORK

First published 1972

Sheed & Ward Inc, 64 University Place, New York, N.Y. 10003
and Sheed & Ward Ltd, 33 Maiden Lane, London WC2E 7LA

Nihil obstat: John M. T. Barton, S.T.D., L.SS
Imprimatur: ✠ Victor Guazzelli, V.G
Westminster, 17 April 1972

Library of Congress Catalog Number 72-2162

This book is set in 12/14 Monotype Imprint

Made and printed in Great Britain by
Billing & Sons Limited, Guildford and London

CONTENTS

Sources and Acknowledgments

"The Sacraments: an Encounter with God" (1957) is from *Christianity Divided*, ed. Daniel J. Callahan and others, New York, Sheed & Ward, 1961; and London, Sheed & Ward, 1962.

"Marriage in the Divine Revelation of the Old Testament" (1963) is from *Marriage: Secular Reality and Saving Mystery*, vol. I, London, Sheed & Ward, 1965; and *Marriage: Human Reality and Saving Mystery*, New York, Sheed & Ward, 1966.

"Revelation, Scripture, Tradition, and Teaching Authority" (1963) is from *Revelation and Theology (Theological Soundings*, vol. I/1), London, Sheed & Ward, 1967; and New York, Sheed & Ward, 1968.

"Secular Worship and Church Liturgy" (1968) is from *God the Future of Man (Theological Soundings*, vol. V/1), New York, Sheed & Ward, 1968; and London, Sheed & Ward, 1969.

INTRODUCTION

The last twenty-five years, and in particular the last ten years, have seen a remarkable flowering of Roman Catholic theology. But for the non-specialist—for the busy parish priest, the active layman, the student—the very wealth of this development presents a range of problems. With which theologian does he begin? Which theologians will he find the most rewarding? Can he ignore any of them?

There are no quick or final answers to such questions, of course, but I hope that this new *Theologians Today* series will help many Catholics to find their own answers more easily. It is designed to achieve two main purposes. Each individual book provides a short but representative introduction to the thought of an outstanding Catholic theologian of the present day, and the series as a whole demonstrates the kind of relationship existing between the best contemporary Catholic theology and official Church teaching.

Both purposes are met by the framework common to all the books. For each book I have selected—and arranged in order of original publication—four pieces which indicate the range in time, approach, and special interest of the theologian concerned. Partly to make my selections more 'objective', but mainly to emphasise the close connection between the theologian's writing and the teaching of Vatican II, I have keyed the articles to the four major documents of that Council—the four Constitutions, on the Church, on Revelation, on the Liturgy, and on the Church in the Modern World.

The selections are very much my own. The theologians themselves, or other editors, would doubtless have made different choices. Nevertheless, I feel that—granted my self-imposed limitations of space and conciliar theme, and the further necessary limitations imposed by copyright or by a proper preference for the out-of-print or inaccessible over the widely available—I have done my own best for men to whom I owe a large debt of gratitude.

The first chapter here is a very useful summary of the main themes of *Christ the Sacrament of the Encounter with God*, probably the most influential of all Edward Schillebeeckx's books. It also illustrates, as in different ways do the three following chapters, one of Prof Schillebeeckx's most important characteristics—his combination of an utter faithfulness to the full biblical, patristic, and medieval tradition of the Church with an openness to all that is positive or illuminating in contemporary thought.

MARTIN REDFERN

8

1. The Sacraments: an Encounter with God

"It is through the sacraments and the exercise of the virtues that the sacred nature and organic structure of the priestly community is brought into operation."— *Dogmatic Constitution on the Church*, II, 11.

The sacramental principle of Revelation

It may be true that Rudolf Bultmann's attempt to demythologize the Christian kerygma, that is, to abandon its objective character and interpret it existentially, is unacceptable. It is true, none the less, that traditional theology has not alway brought out clearly enough the distinction between the mere physical presence (*Vorhandensein*) of the things of nature and the unique character of conscious human reality (*Dasein*) and human existence (*Existenz*). The personal call which the living God addresses to man in his human situation often seems endangered by a reduction of religious life to the impersonal level. And it was precisely in the theology of the sacraments that this kind of approach resulted in treating sacramental life too exclusively as an impersonal cause–effect relationship. This led to the idea that our reception of grace in the sacraments is mainly a passive affair.

Our aim in this present work is to throw some light on the essential sacramental character of the Church from the standpoint of *intersubjectivity* or *existential personal encounter*. Religion, after all, is a dialogue between God and man. By his created powers man can reach God only through the medium of his creation as its First Cause. At the utmost, all man can do is arouse only a powerless longing for the person of the living God (in reality, the three Persons) and for the immediacy of an I–Thou relationship with him. But by reason of the gratuitous, saving initiative of the living God, the religious man finds himself in direct converse with his God. In this divine encounter or personal fellowship with God—called saving grace —consists *salvation*. This encounter is, from God's side, *revelation;* from man's side, his *religious response.*

Revelation and religion—or, in other words, the mutual encounter of man, created and situated in history, with the uncreated God—of their very nature create history and hence, in the widest sense of the word, are truly sacramental. We call sacramental every supernatural saving reality which presents itself in our lives historically. God directs what he plans for man through history, and he does it in such a way that his interventions can be recognized by men as divine. God's giving grace to man makes history by revealing itself, and it reveals itself by becoming history.

Precisely because the supernatural saving reality, veiled in historical events, and surrounded by the darkness of mystery, is present to us only in earthly form (*sacramentum*), it demands the revealing word (*verbum*) as the interior aspect of its earthly appearance. Only in and through the prophetic word is the divine dimension of saving history brought to light. "Word" and "sacrament" are therefore the fundamental constituents for revelation in the Old Testament as well as in the New and, after this revelation has been brought to an end, for the life of the Church which grows out of it.

Christianity as personal communion of man with the living God in Christ

Intersubjectivity or the dialogue structure of revelation (as "Word and sacrament") appears already in the Old Testament. Yahweh is the God of the Covenant. He personally intervenes in favour of the one determined people he himself has freely chosen out of the community of nations—Israel. He intervenes *personally*, not just as the Creator who by his power guides the historical course of all nations in creative transcendence, but as one who takes part in the vicissitudes of history and who stands on the side of Israel. The core of Israel's history, as it was interpreted through the prophetic word, is set forth over and over again in the Old Testament as: "I will be *your* God, you *my* people" (Lev 26:11–12; Jer 7:23; 11:4; 24:7; 31:33; Ezek 11:20; 14:11; 37:27; Hos 1:9; etc.).

The burden of all God's revelation in the Old Testament is exactly the course of history which results from the alternation between God's constant fidelity and the ever-recurring infidelity of his people. This revelation, then, is accomplished in a dialectical situation: Out of the dialogue struggle between God and his people, in fidelity and infidelity, the concrete content of revelation takes shape. In one way, of course, this arises from a decision of the living God which is completely and sovereignly free. But looked at from the viewpoint of history, this revelation remains the result of a dialogue of acts: between the invitation and proposal of love by God and the personal, loving response or refusal of love by God's people.

Through all the vicissitudes of this history God desires to lead his people in spite of everything to a final and definitive fidelity. This intention of God appears to be a failure—at least for the majority: the Jews reject their Messiah. The revelation which leads up to Christ then, evolves in history as a dialogue in which God wrestles with human freedom in his desire to save mankind. It is an existential, two-way struggle between God who calls and man who resists —until this God who invites to a faithful love, himself personally responds as true man to this courtship, with a return of love whose fidelity knows no bounds —which does not shrink even from the death of the Cross.

In the man Jesus is realized the fidelity of the covenant in a twofold way. At last the dialogue which was ever breaking down finds a full and perfect human resonance. In a single person both elements are fulfilled: the invitation, and the reply of perfect fidelity, and in such a way that both the invitation and the response constitute the completed revelation of God.

The Sacraments: an Encounter with God

The man Jesus is not only the one sent by the Holy Trinity, he is also the one called to be the representative of all humanity. He is not only the visible embodiment of God's wooing of man, but also the representation and highest fulfilment of the human response of love to God's courtship. Jesus, the free man, who in his humanity reveals to us the divine invitation of love, is at the same time, as man, the person who in the name of all of us and as our representative accepts this invitation. As head of redeemed humanity, he is in a sense the whole of mankind. That is why it is possible for his sacrifice to be at the same time our redemption. Only by uniting ourselves to the man Jesus does our own personal fidelity to the covenant become possible. Our personal communion with God can only take place, explicitly or implicitly, by an interpersonal relationship with the man Jesus.

Sacramental encounter with God through encounter with the man Jesus

The encounter of man with the invisible God through the medium of the visible embodiment of the love of that same God in a man we call a *sacramental encounter with God*. To be personally addressed by the man Jesus is for the believer personal encounter with God; for God himself, the eternal Logos, is *personally* this man. Whoever touches with faith the hem of Christ's garment is immediately healed. That is why the human interchange, the interpersonal

15

relationship between Jesus and the men he encounters, is the sacrament of their encounter with
God. It means grace and redemption for all who in
living faith actually come face to face with the man
Jesus.

Social intercourse between men, however, occurs
through and in bodily forms. Spiritual influence on
a fellow man requires bodily means of communication; it remains a human activity which must find its
bodily expression. Jesus was a real man. He was the
Son of God appearing in a truly human form, an
incarnated human spirit. His contacts with other men
required, as do every man's, bodily means of
communication. Nevertheless, the encounter of
Christ with his fellow men and his properly human
activity remain a personal deed of the Son of God,
although in human form. It is consequently a divine
encounter with men in a truly human form. And as
the activity of the Son of God, this encounter of
Christ as man with men possesses divine saving
power; it is the friendship of God himself for man,
translated and transformed into the form of human
encounter. Although this is true of every truly human
activity of Christ, it is especially true of those human
actions of Christ which are exclusively actions of
God, although accomplished in a human manner,
that is, his miracles and, more especially, redemption
itself which finds its consummation in the sacrifice of
the Cross.

But since the translation of God's encounter with
man into an encounter between men includes bodily

elements making it visible, this human encounter of Christ with his fellow men possesses not only *divine* saving power in a very general way (since it is a personal action of the Son of God) but divine saving power which is specifically *sacramental;* for the human actions of Jesus in their visibility and corporality are the human outward manifestation of the divine bestowal of grace. They are "signs and causes" of grace, and this in such fashion that the same reality which is externally visible (the sign) is the inner saving power itself in visible form: the concrete embodiment of the offering of grace.

That the human actions of Jesus have sacramental saving efficacy in themselves means, finally, that our "body–spirit" encounter with the man Jesus is the sacrament of our encounter with God. And because redemption through the man Jesus is achieved "once and for all", and in such a way that every communication of grace remains essentially bound up with this man, therefore, every bestowal of grace or encounter with God will come about in an encounter with this man Jesus. The intersubjective relationship of the believer with Christ, the primordial sacrament (*Ursakrament*), remains the basic event of the Christian religion as personal communion with the three divine persons.

Sacramental encounter with Christ as the full development of religious encounter with God

In the appearance of the man Christ, the anonymity of the living God is removed. The man Jesus shows us the true face of the living God in such a way that the universal religious themes come to the fore only in Christ. For in fact God reveals himself not only interiorly through his mysterious appeal to our souls (the impulse of the Holy Spirit drawing us to belief); he has, as we have said, concretized his inner invitation to personal communion with him in saving history and (fully at last) in the human appearance of Christ in this world. God desired not only to be God for us, he wanted to be God for us in a *human* way. For the first time we can fully grasp what sanctifying grace means; how it reveals, on the one hand, God's boundless desire for a personal communion with us, for the man Jesus who longs to befriend us is precisely revelation of God. On the other hand, it also reveals how profoundly meant our human response to that divine love ought to be, for the man Jesus whose devoted, childlike intimacy with his Father remaining faithful even unto death is also a vicarious realization of our devotion, the highest realization of religious intimacy with the living God which man has ever undertaken.

The bodily manifestation of divine life through Christ's human soul, the incarnation, also plays a decisive role in solving the mystery of God's anonymity in the world. That its sacramental character

18

makes Christianity the perfect form of religious life can be elucidated from insights into the true nature of man.

The human body is not only the appearance and countenance of the human person who reveals himself, it is also that in which and by which the soul develops into a fully-fledged person. To join both ideas together: in and through the body the soul externalizes its process of becoming a person. By going out into the world, the human person gains self-consciousness. It is only in incarnation, becoming-flesh, that personal activity is completed. Thus, embodiment serves as the sign, although a sign that also veils, of the most intimate personal activity.

The point here is that dynamic personality constitutes itself in and through an activity which externalizes itself also in bodily form. In the body the soul presents itself to another. "What we in encounter call body is that through which we situate ourselves, express ourselves, and make ourselves known; in short, the form of man's being-in-the-world. The person we encounter *has* this form, but he also *is* this form."[1] It is through the body and in the body that human encounter takes place. In virtue of this, human relationships of a spiritual nature, no matter how independent they are in themselves of bodily encounter, nevertheless do attain their high points in such an encounter because in it the spiritual interrelationship is made fully present.

Of course, we should by no means overlook the unique characteristic of the man Christ. He is truly

God-man, divine in a human way and human in a divine way. Nonetheless, he is truly man. What we have said about the human dimension pertains also to Christ in his personal relations with his fellow men. For the apostles, the moments of their companionship with Christ in both soul *and* body were the decisive high points of their experience of Christ. The Last Supper is a typical example; or Jesus' glance to Peter after his denial, which was enough to move him to tears.

In such bodily–spiritual encounters Christ himself makes the gift of his presence an intensely vivid reality, while in those also bodily encounters the disciples experience their spiritual bond with Christ more deeply than ever. On both sides the bodily personal encounter is the point at which spiritual encounter culminates. And since the spiritual intervention of the man Jesus, the redeeming God, is an intervention in grace, this means that the sacramentalizing or the embodying of this gracious intervention is the culmination of Christ's will to bestow grace and bring salvation. Conversely, whoever in faith encounters the man Jesus and is offered his mercy in a visible and tangible form can achieve through this a fully developed religious attitude.

In the encounter with Christ the anonymity of man's experience of God is removed. In religions outside Christianity man cannot normally reach to an experience of God except in a vague and often nameless way. It is only in the sacramental encounter with Christ that this experience of God can develop into a mature and fully personal religious worship. The full unfolding of religious life has, therefore, a sacramental basis: the primordial sacrament (*Ursakrament*), Christ Jesus.

Against this one could object: Christ himself has said that "the Spirit gives life, the flesh is of no avail" (Jn 6:63); or, better: "It is to your advantage that I go away, for if I do not go away, the Counsellor will not come to you" (Jn 16:7). The corporal absence of Christ seems to be the very thing which ushers in the perfection of religious life.

It is true, of course, that Christ had to go where we cannot yet follow him. He rose and vanished out of our visible world of empirical experience. But it is not his invisibility as such that "is good for us", but his *glorification* out of death. For us, this necessarily involves his withdrawal because we have not yet been glorified ourselves. But this means precisely that the definitive, eternal, and unsurpassable fulfilment both of the incarnation and of our religious life takes place there where we ourselves enjoy the privilege of being together with Christ in transfigured *bodily* form, after his return. From this very fact it is clear that our earthly Christian life and (since this life, as we will see, demands sacraments) our sacramental life must fundamentally be an eschatological advance toward the Parousia. What at first seemed an objection, in reality confirms our position; precisely since the fullness of religious worship can only be realized in the sacramental, bodily–spiritual encounter with Christ, therefore Christianity, as the life which elapses between Pasch and Parousia, is fundamentally eschatological. In the last analysis the saying of Tertullian proves true: "*Caro salutis est cardo*" (It is on the flesh that salvation hinges).[2]

The sacraments of the Church as human encounter with the glorified Kyrios (Lord)

Another objection may perhaps be raised: Must we who have never encountered Christ in the flesh and who have not yet been taken up in glory—must we manage to get along meanwhile without bodily encounter with Christ? Must our Christ–encounter occur in a purely mystical fashion, in the purely spiritual contact of faith, as our Protestant brothers in the faith suppose? The first answer that suggests itself is: in a certain sense, yes; just as those of the Old Covenant and also the other non-Jewish and non-Christian religions had to and still have to get along without any bodily encounter with Christ, although all of these were and are already indebted to Christ for everything. This makes Catholic life fundamentally a life of *waiting:* "awaiting our blessed hope" (Titus 2:13). Our eschatological eagerness is a vigil, an advance toward a meeting, an encounter not yet complete. Christianity is the religion of *Maranatha:* "Come, Lord Jesus!" (Rev 22:20); "Thy Kingdom come!" (Mt 6:10; Lk 11:2).

But this is only one aspect. This active expectation of the perfect encounter is not sustained merely through an encounter with Christ which is only spiritual, or achieved through a mystical act of faith; but it is sustained just as much through an encounter with the living *Kyrios* (Lord) which, though unique, is nevertheless real and quasi-bodily—this encounter takes place in the sacraments of the Church and through them. And this quasi-bodily or strictly sacramental encounter with Christ is for that very reason a pledge and anticipation of the eschatological and perfect encounter with Christ.

From behind the cloud of his glorification, behind which he withdraws from our still earthly eyes, the Lord in his visible Church reaches for earthly, unglorified elements which for that very reason are visible to us, elements as unpretentious as the child in the crib: a little bread and wine, oil and water, a warm, fatherly hand upon the forehead, in order to make his heavenly, saving act effectively present to us here and now. The Church's sacraments are, therefore, our quasi-bodily encounters with the transfigured man Jesus, a veiled contact with the Lord but, none the less, one which is concretely human in the full sense because both body and soul are involved. Therefore, based on the historical redemptive event of Christ who is himself the *Eschaton*, the sacramental encounter is a celebration in mystery of the Parousia.

From this we see the "why" of the Church's sacraments. The man Jesus, the visible, fully human image of the redeeming God is, as we have said, the "once-for-all" sacramental sign in which the mystery of the divine redeeming love is visibly represented to us and through which the redeeming God introduces us into existential, personal communion with himself. Since the Ascension has withdrawn the man Jesus from the visible horizon of our lives, our encounter with the living Lord Christ, our perennial mediator, would take place purely mystically by faith if there were no sacraments. Irremediably one of the human dimensions of the Incarnation would in fact be lost for all of us who have never encountered Christ in his earthly life. But God has remained true to his pedagogy. With sympathetic consideration for the characteristic situation of the human person who, because of his bodily nature, lives in a world of men and things, and reaches spiritual maturity in them and through them, God ever offers us the kingdom of Heaven in earthly garb. Thus it was in the days of the covenant; thus it was at the *ephapax* (once and for all: Heb 9:12) of the human appearance of the redeeming God; and this is what the divine pedagogy requires now in the sacramental Church which is the earthly, visible instrument of salvation employed by the living, invisible *Kyrios*.

The divine plan of salvation is essentially a sacramental economy of salvation. It is true that the spiritual Christ can meet us and influence our lives outside the sacramental visibility of the Church. None the less, *by reason of his glorified body*, he can only make himself *fully present for us and to us* (and thus exploit his grace-giving approach to the full) by using earthly, untransfigured elements as visible symbols, prolonging and manifesting his invisible, heavenly, saving act. The concrete presence of this

24

heavenly saving activity of Christ demands that the *Kyrios* embody his invisible, saving efficacy in this earthly world by employing unglorified corporeality which becomes an interior element of his heavenly, symbolic action. The sacramentalism of the Church bridges the disproportion between our untransfigured world and the Christ: the world, that is, which at one point, at its centre, is already glorified.

In the context of the historical milieu in which we live, the sacraments are a visible expression of the celestial, present, saving action of Christ, the *Eschaton*. In the sacraments we encounter Christ, though he be bodily absent, in a tangible, bodily way. The Eucharist is for us the crowning point of this actual encounter with Christ.

Thus we see immediately that the so-called *sacramenta separata* (separated sacraments) are not things, but rather personal encounters with the glorified man Jesus and in him with the living God. We now wish to investigate, first, the objective structure of these sacraments, and then reflect on the religious spirit in which we personally should celebrate them.

The sacraments of the Church

The man Jesus himself is the primordial sacrament (*Ursakrament*). The redemption wrought through him is "once for all" and conclusive. The sacraments of the Church have no new and additional meaning; they merely bring us in their own way into living contact with the "perennial Christ", who through the

25

power of the Holy Spirit remains the permanent mediator between the Father and men. The sacraments of the Church, consequently, rest on an essentially Christological foundation: "For there is no other Sacrament of God but Christ."[3]

If the sacraments of the Church are only the points of contact on earth with Christ the primordial sacrament (*Ursakrament*), that means that they *sacramentalize* the redeeming work of Christ for us and in us here and now: "What was visible in Christ passed over into the sacraments of the Church."[4] The significance of the Christological dimension of the sacraments can be made clear only after we have explained their ecclesiological basis.

(*a*) *The ecclesiological dimension of the sacraments.* We have already said that in God's economy of salvation the man Jesus represents the whole human race. In the sense of being its origin, he himself, as head of the human race he has redeemed, is personally the Church. In the fullest sense of the word this means that in the sacrifice of the Cross of Jesus, the whole human race became "Church". "Christ died so that by His death might arise the Church."[5] Christ's sacrifice on the Cross has meaning as a real fact only if it is at the same time the sign of the sacrifice of all mankind; and it has this value as a representative sign effectively only to the extent that it is at the same time a real fact. In this respect the Church exists only in germ, that is, in the representative humanity of Jesus, sacrificed, yet glorified.

The Sacraments: an Encounter with God

The earthly Church is the sign, present within the world, of this victorious and definitive redemption which introduces the *Eschaton*. When we spoke of the sacraments as that which makes present in the world in earthly garb the saving action of Christ in glory, we meant, first of all, the sacramental *Church* itself. It is the visible, historical representation in the world of the definitive redemption. Christianity is essentially a belief in earthly realities as the appearance in mystery of the supernatural realities of the redemption.

Accordingly, the Church as the institution of salvation is essentially sacrament and Word. Both form the specific area of endeavour for the hierarchical ministry. The norm for ministry, sacrament, and Word is, on the one hand, the *ephapax* (once-and-for-all character) of the historical appearance of Christ and of the apostolic, primitive tradition, and on the other hand the earthly form of the saving action of the glorified *Kyrios* through his Spirit. The whole visible Church is ruled by the glorified *Kyrios* who, through the mediation both of his Holy Spirit and of the apostolic ministry of his earthly Church, brings to completion in this world the building up of the people of God. Christ *sends* the Holy Spirit (Jn 14:16, 26; 15:26) and he also *sends* his apostles (Jn 13:16, 20; 17:18). Both of these sendings are organically connected with one another. Pentecost, the day on which the Church with its sacramental and kerygmatic activity stepped forth into the full light of day, is the mystery event of the manifestation of both these missions precisely in their conjointly acting unity, a unity which is vitalized from a single source of life, the *Kyrios* himself. What the visible Church does in the order of historical, external visibility, the Spirit sent by Christ does interiorly both in the Church's authorized ministers and in the souls of the faithful. That is why the Church as the representation of the mystery of Christ can herself be called a primordial sacrament (*Ursakrament*) insofar as it is (1) *sacramentum humanitatis Christi* (sacrament of the humanity of Christ) or the sacramental Christ, and (2) the subject in which the seven sacraments, the specific ministerial actions of the sacramental Church, are found.

This means that the seven sacraments, even before they are this or that particular sacrament, are first of all and primarily the visible official action of the Church or, better, the action of Christ in heaven sacramentalized in the visible action of the Church. They are the activity of the *Church* from a sevenfold perspective. This is the reason why the power of orders and the power of jurisdiction are interwoven in every sacrament and why the validity of an action of the power of orders can be limited, altered, or nullified by the power of jurisdiction. The validity or authentic sacramentality of the seven sacraments, therefore, fundamentally depends on whether or not the sacrament in question is truly an action of the Church of Christ. The so-called "matter" and "form" point out two complementary ways of giving concrete form to the ecclesial character of this celebration in

28

mystery, which being "sacrament" includes "sacramental Word" as an inner constituent because the supernatural dimension of the earthly event is only made fully present to us in the Word.

The primary aspect, which reveals itself in a variety of shadings, in the reception of each of the seven sacraments, is the setting up of living contact with the visible Church in the actions as Christ's representative which are characteristic of her as the Church. It is precisely this visible contact with the Church through the reception of its sacraments in faith that *is* the encounter with Christ.

This already implies that the *main* lines of this economy of the seven sacraments were established by Christ when he founded the Church. The fullness of the gift of redemption is bound up, through Christ's founding of the Church, with the great external sign: the Church as the historical reality which renders the achieved redemption present. Thus, Christ's founding of his Church as primordial sacrament (*Ursakrament*) is basically also the institution of the seven sacraments. What the sacraments do is nothing more than make concretely present here and now what the Church itself is in its essence. True enough, Christ himself also said, implicitly or explicitly, that the sevenfold treasure of the grace of redemption should be shared in through the visible activity of the Church. But apart from the fact that for a few sacraments he himself also determined the outer form of the visible action (e.g. washing with *water*, the sacrifice of *bread* and *wine*), he gave full scope to the

Church to determine for itself the external symbolic form of its visible action which would be the outward sign of the sevenfold sacramental grace. But the fundamental and decisive factor, the joining of the sevenfold grace to a visible action of the Church— *that* comes directly from Christ. The *substantia sacramenti* (essential element of a sacrament)—that element in the external sign which cannot be changed by the Church[6] and hence was determined by Christ himself—signifies, simply, the sacramental meaning as expressed in external form, that is, the sacramentalizing of a sevenfold grace. (With regard to certain sacraments this can also involve the concrete determination of the external symbolic form.)

The fact that the sacramental meaning is expressed in an *action* of the Church implies, as we have said, that it has as an intimate constituent element the sacramental Word. It is this alone that makes fully present to us in a visible action the supernatural saving presence. Both together—the liturgical action joined to the sacramental Word of the Church, made one in the liturgy—are the elements which go to make up the external symbolic action of the Church and turn it into a sacrament where we meet Christ. The sacraments are, therefore, the specifically churchly actions which make visible on earth the fulfilled messianic activity of her high priest in heaven.

That there are *seven* sacraments derives, in the last analysis, exclusively from the saving will of Christ. But this number seven should be explained not so much anthropologically, through an analogy with human life on a biological level, as ecclesiologically, i.e. from the essence of the Church as the kingdom of God existing on earth in historical form. For the sevenfold sacramental grace is the grace of redemption which comes to us in visible form, in the seven dimensions presented us by the Church. The fundamental reality which takes on a special shading in each of the seven sacraments is the personal contact with the inner dynamism of the holy Church, which contact itself is the effective sign of our personal encounter with the glorified man Jesus and in him with the living God. The special symbolism of each sacrament's liturgical action, taken as a whole in which the Word elucidates the symbol, highlights that special aspect under which the one redeeming action of Christ reaches us in the Church through the various sacraments.

On this account it is the progressive realization of the kingdom of God in each individual person and in the human race as a whole which demands a sevenfold, sacramental saving activity of the Church.

(*b*) *The christological content of the sacraments of the Church.* The necessity of the sacraments is based upon the fact that grace continues to be mediated through the man Jesus. Since Christ's ascension, this further continuation demands, as we have seen, the introduction of the sacramental Church with its sacramental activity (*sacramenta separata*) in which this mediation of grace visibly enters into our earthly

31

world. Therefore, even after the ascension, the conferring of grace continues to be on the basis of intersubjectivity between us men and the man Jesus, which is the sacrament of our personal fellowship with God. Since the ascension, the perfect form of this intersubjectivity with the man Jesus takes place only within the sacred domain of the Church of Christ. This proposes for us the problem of "presence in mystery" (*Mysteriengegenwart*). Without allowing ourselves to become involved in the numerous and various opinions concerning this theory which have grown out of the discussion of the work of Dom Odo Casel, nor in the problem of what exactly Casel meant to affirm, we present a solution which immediately suggests itself from the standpoint of a sound Christology.

To put it in terms of time: When God became man, the eternal Redeemer entered into time. Now time is irreversible. What has happened historically can, in no way, be made actual again, not even by God. As an historical incident it is irrevocably past. Since, therefore, Christ was *really* man, the sacrifice of the Cross as an historical event is also a reality that is past; and it cannot actually be made to be present again even "in mystery". Of course, it is true that an historical action of a human person, being a personal action, in a certain respect surpasses time because it is a *spiritual* act and it had a part in fashioning the person into what he now is. But this does not alter the fact that the historical element of that act as a human act belongs irrevocably to the past and as

32

such it can no longer be made actually present, not even in a mysterious way. The past of the human acts of Jesus inescapably shares in this irreversibility of the time event, otherwise we fall into a kind of Docetism.

On the other hand, the historical human acts of Christ, who is personally God, are the *personal* acts of the second divine Person, even though performed through his humanity. Therefore, Jesus' sacrifice on the Cross, as a personal action of God, is an eternally present actuality which is imperishable. The sacrifice of the Cross, not in its historical form as human act, which proceeds from the *Son of God* who *personalizes* the *human* act of Jesus—this sacrifice of the Cross, in its inner nature a truly divine act of sacrifice (although performed in the humanity and therefore in time) is—as is everything which is divine—eternal, and not past. Redemption, therefore, if considered *exclusively* as an action of God (only God can redeem us), is, although achieved in this humanity, an eternally present divine act. The death on the Cross, then, itself possesses a "mystery" content which transcends time.

Since Jesus did not cease to be man after the Resurrection but remains man, we must also speak of the *permanence* or perennial character of the *Kyrios:* "Christ yesterday and today and for ever!" (Heb 13:8). To be sure, the eternally present redemptive act has in itself a "changing" human mode of expression—a "movement" which we, of course, cannot measure by earthly time because it is the human act of a man who has risen and shares in the vision of God. There is a difference between the mode of expression in the historical sacrifice on the Cross and in the Christ in glory. The historical human mode of appearance of the inner act of sacrifice of the Son of God is for ever past; but it remains in its mystery content as an action of God. It possesses an eternal contemporaneity in the now living Christ, in whom it becomes humanly incarnate in a new "heavenly" manner. Rooted in an act of God, the death on the Cross has, therefore, an eternally permanent content, a content which had us in view in the sacrificial death and which still presents itself to us now.

The man Jesus is in a glorified state and is for that reason (to us) invisible. We, on the other hand, find ourselves in an untransfigured earthly condition. Consequently, the eternally-present redemptive act of the sacrifice of the Cross indeed can have a direct influence on us, but it can no longer be made present to us "in Christ's own body". The eternally-present divine redemption consummated in human nature can be rendered present now, as has been shown, only through sacramental, earthly symbols, especially those of the Eucharist. From this it automatically follows that there is inescapably a "presence in mystery" in the seven sacraments—and in a very special way for the Eucharist.

The whole redeeming mystery of Christ, not in some way or other in its historical content, but as the act of God, becomes actively present in the sacra-

34

ments, so that in these sacraments we are immediately encompassed by the redemptive efficacy of the "redeeming Incarnation". It thus becomes clear that the core of the sacramental efficacy is the eternally-present act of redemption of the Son of God; and that this is *identical* with both the mystery content of the saving action of the historical sacrifice of the Cross and with the mystery content of the saving activity of the living, glorified *Kyrios* and, finally, with the mystery of the saving power of the sacramental Church; although in all of this the *human* form given to the divine redeeming act of the man Jesus is different in each case. From this viewpoint the *ephapax* and the sufficiency of the historical event of redemption is shown to be in no way threatened or cancelled out by the sacraments of the Church; and it becomes clear that to support this we do not have to call on the questionable theory which says that a past, temporal event can be made somehow actual again in our own time *in mysterio* or in some "mystical" way.

Yet for all this the sacraments are truly also a celebration in mystery of the past *acta et passa Christi* (actions and sufferings of Christ) and always contain a reference to the historical coming of Christ. For on the Cross—and *only* there—at that historical moment, God offered for us his human life. Therefore, the eternally-present redemptive act of God retains a reference to the past sacrifice on the Cross. The eternally-present redemptive act of the Son of God made man is actively made present in the sacraments precisely as referring to the historical sacrifice of the Cross. That is why St Thomas says with all Tradition that the sacraments draw their saving power from the death of Christ. We must maintain at the same time, however, that it is the glorified Christ now living who gives to the sacraments their saving efficacy. "It is Christ himself, through his Church baptizes, teaches, rules, absolves, makes sacrifice."[7]

The sacraments as a medium between Christ and us should be situated, then, not so much between the historically past sacrifice of the Cross and our present situation in the twentieth century, as between the now living, glorified Christ, the *Eschaton*, and our own human world which is not yet transfigured and which strains toward the *Eschaton*. In other words, we should conceive of the sacraments as a "medium" in a real encounter *between living men:* between the man Jesus and us men and, therefore, *as this very encounter itself.* For although personal encounter through the medium of the body in a certain respect is indirect, it is, nevertheless, also *immediate* since in the body subjectivity immediately and directly expresses itself.

It is only this encounter with Christ in and through the actual presence in the sacraments of the eternally-present redemptive act of the living Christ (and of the redeeming Christ himself in the Eucharist) which explains the historical perspective in the sacraments insofar as they are: (1) an *anamnesis* (commemoration) or celebration in mystery of the past sacrifice of the Cross (*signum rememorativum*), because precisely at the sacrifice of the Cross the eternally-present redemptive act of the Son of God amounted to really giving up his life; (2) *actual bestowal of grace* (*signum demonstrativum*), because the receiving subject is here and now really drawn into the eternally-present redemptive act; (3) an *anticipation*, in germ, of the eschatological Parousia (*signum prognosticum*), because they are the sacramental act of rendering the *Eschaton* itself present (in the Eucharist) or at least of making present the eternally-actual redemptive act of the Son of God in his efficacy as the glorified *Kyrios* (in the other six sacraments); they allow our own time to be grasped in a visible way by the *Eschaton* itself. The sacramental encounter of man with Christ in the Church is, therefore, on the basis of the historically-past redeeming event, the beginning or the *arrha* (pledge) here and now of eschatological salvation; and the supporting substratum of all this is the permanence of the redeeming man Jesus, who is God and who, through his sacraments, receives us into his redeeming mercy.

Sacramental mystery of worship and sacramental sanctification

In the concrete, the man Jesus is not only the person who offers us in this humanity the grace of God; he is also the person who in his humanity as our representative and in our name in obedient religious love accepts the offer of grace. Tradition expresses this by saying: "The man Jesus *gives* us the grace that as man he *merited* for us on the Cross." In the saving acts of Christ we find, therefore, a double aspect: worship for God and sanctification for man. These are two aspects of the same *mysteria carnis Christi* (mysteries of Christ's flesh). This idea must now be further developed.

Even to the very core of what is most human in him, Jesus is the Son of God the Father. In grace, therefore, he enjoys the perfection of the intimacy with the three-in-one God. He is the consummate actualization of the communion of love of man with God. He is "grace become man": As God-man, he is essentially dialogue between the holy man Jesus and the Father in the unity of the Holy Spirit. As God, Christ is the second Person, the Son of God, in all things like to the Father. "Living because of the Father" (Jn 6:57), receiving all things from him, the Son is nevertheless true God and, in this sense, not "dependent" on the Father. There is question here of an intimacy by which (without prejudice to full equality) the Father is the source without origin. We find ourselves, then, before the incomprehensible mystery of a divine and, therefore, "independent" person Who, nevertheless, "derives" from the Father and possesses all things from him (derivation of origin without proper dependence) *a Patre* and *ad Patrem* (from the Father and to the Father).

Now the *human existence* of Jesus is the revelation of this divine inner-trinitarian life relationship: its translation into human forms of appearance. What is translated on to a human level in the man Jesus is primarily this divine intimacy of love of the Son for His Father. In the humanity of the Son the divine intimacy of love between Son and Father is brought to the *created* level, and thus in the man Jesus a real dependence toward the Father now comes into existence *in* this loving intimacy of the Son become man. "The Father is greater than I" (Jn 14:28). In and through this condition the Son reveals to us his divine loving intimacy with the Father—to the "principle without origin". The "being-from-the-Father" of the Son is made known to us by the man Jesus in His *obedient* or *dependent* love for the Father. The man Jesus is essentially *obedient* love and adoration of the Father as the human translation of his divine relationship of origin. Thus considered, the whole earthly life of Jesus is spent before the Father in "living out" this childhood which he acquired by becoming man. In obedient love for his Father, he has accepted his whole human existence (*Dasein*) which, through the intrigues of his fellow men, ended in his being murdered, as the religious expression of his ever-unshaken devotion to his Father. Through this supreme religious worship of Christ we have been redeemed.

But Christ reveals to us through and in his humanity not only his divine relationship to his Father but also his relationship to the Holy Spirit. The Son of God is also a *coprinciple of the Holy Spirit*: "who proceeds from the Father through the Son." The mission of the Holy Spirit *to us* is also the externalizing of this inner trinitarian structure.

The "from the Father through the Son" as expressed in the Incarnation signifies that the Holy Spirit is given to us from the Father in and through the perfection of the Son's religiously obedient love (the human level of divine filiation as *a Patre* and *ad Patrem*). That is why John twice mentions that Christ could send us the Holy Spirit only after his resurrection from the dead (Jn 16:7; 7:37–39; see also Acts 2:33). Theology says the same when it tells us that Jesus through his human life has *merited* for us the Holy Spirit. Only with the final closing, the crowning of his earthly obedient life, is the "incarnation" concluded; only then is the *a Patre* and *ad Patrem* character of the Son fully translated on the human level. "Into thy hands I commend my spirit" is the consummate incarnational translation of the "*ad Patrem*" which is the Son. The Father's responding acceptance of his Son—on the level of the incarnation—is the resurrection and ascension which concludes the cycle of loving intimacy between the Father and the Son become man. Only now can the Son—who on the trinitarian level in his "*ad Patrem*" is the coprinciple of the Holy Spirit—only now can he on the level of the incarnation send the Holy Spirit to us, too. Thus, through the worship mystery of his life which culminated in death, the man Jesus "merited" for us "*the spirit* of sonship" (Rom 8:15); and thus he effectively bestows on us, as *Kyrios*, his own Spirit.

In this primordial sacrament (*Ursakrament*) which is Christ himself, who is personally God, we see that the redemptive act is a *mystery of worship* which is *liturgical* because it was done in our name (*leiton* or *laiton ergon* [work of the people], and at the same time is the gift of redemption or *sanctification*. Both are achieved by God in human nature.

We find these two aspects again in the sacraments of the Church as celebrations in mystery of the Redemption; in them the Church celebrates the "mysteries of Christ's flesh", a liturgical mystery of worship in which Christ in and through the Church remains the actual high priest. In and through his Church, Christ sacramentalizes his intercession for us in heaven. It is the way he as Lord manifests his eternally-present divine redeeming act, so that every sacrament that is performed for one of the faithful is a *sacramental prayer for grace* for this believer: the prayer of Christ himself to which the Church joins its prayer here and now (*sacramenta fidei Ecclesiae*— sacraments of the faith of the Church). On the other hand, the sacraments are also the sacramentalizing of Christ's *effective sanctification* from heaven in and through his Holy Spirit. In virtue of the eternally-present redeeming act of the *Kyrios*, both efficacious and an act of worship, the sacraments *bestow* the grace which they *ask* of God by this act of worship.

Thus the sacraments of the Church give grace because the Church itself is visibly and perceptibly full of grace. It is, after all, the historical, tangible presence of the redeeming grace of the Cross here and now in the world. In its sacramental activity the Church is not only the effective instrument of salvation employed by the living *Kyrios* by which he establishes on earth among men a community in faith and love (i.e. the Church as a community in grace) and interiorly intensifies and deepens the life of its members, but this visible sacramental expression also makes visible the inner community of faith and grace of *the ever-holy Church* itself. The Church is community of worship and community of sanctification in such a way that in the very act of giving expression to its holiness in sacramental worship it is seen to be *carrying on the work itself of sanctification.* The grace which operates in the sacraments is Christ's fullness of grace shared in his living Church. The sacraments, therefore, are not only the saving sign of the sanctifying worship of Christ, but no less the worship of the Church itself, the expression of the Church's life of grace as community with Christ. The *pleroma Christi* (fullness of Christ) operates in each sacrament. In and through the performance of a sacrament, Christ and his whole Church surround with prayer the man who receives the sacrament. "The *faith* of the Church contributes to the efficacy of baptism," a faith which is always vivified by charity.[8] In every sacrament the believer enters more deeply into the living bond which the community of the Church has with the "mysteries of Christ's flesh". The mystery of worship, precisely because of its sacramentality, is not only the worship of Christ himself in and through his Church, but by the very fact a *liturgical* mystery of worship of the Church: the liturgical expression of the inner worship of God by the Church's

42

community of the faithful in union with Christ. All this belongs to the constitution of a *sacrament* considered *valid* by the Church and which, consequently, if the receiving subject sets up no obstacle—i.e. if the recipient also joins himself in a religious spirit with faith to this mystery of worship—through the very fact of the liturgical celebration (*ex opere operato*), efficaciously bestows the grace prayed for in this act of liturgical worship.

From this we can see the meaning of the traditional formula *Sacramenta causant quod figurant* (the sacraments cause the grace to which they give visible expression). As distinguished from the holy humanity of Jesus, which is hypostatically united to the Son of God, the sacraments are *sacramenta separata*, i.e. earthly manifestations in symbolic signs of the invisible, saving act of the man Jesus in heaven. They are truly, therefore, the personal acts of the God-man in and through the minister of the Church. They are, in visible sacramental form (*signum*), the redeeming will of Christ himself with respect to the man who receives them. The eternally-present redemptive act as designed for us personally is sacramentalized by the glorified Christ in and through his Church. Essentially, therefore, this visible proof of Christ's redemptive love is meant for the believer to whom it is directed: the receiver of the sacrament. That it be directed to this definite man belongs to the essence of a sacramental proof of Christ's love.

Because they are the visible appearance on earth of this celestial saving act, the sacraments have, as a natural consequence, the same divine saving efficacy. The earthly symbolism of the Church visibly represents the heavenly salvific activity. If we consider the sacraments "from below", we can say that they are symbolic acts of worship of the Church in which Christ accomplishes a deeper mystery. Seen thus, the symbolic acts of the Church are *charged* with divine saving efficacy. But if we look at the sacraments "from above", from the standpoint of the saving act in heaven which is sacramentalized in the Church, as the personal human act of Christ through the official mediation of the Church, then the sacraments are the visibility in the Church, or the historical "incarnation", of the sanctifying will of Christ; they are this saving will itself in visible and tangible form. And thus because of their sacramental visibility, they are the effective bestowal itself of grace made manifest in a visible and therefore meaningful way. Just as the body is the soul itself made visible (but in such a way that the proper activity of the body can in no way be made equivalent to the spiritual activity of the soul), so also at Baptism, for example, the corporal washing of the Church is the divine grace of reconciliation made visible on earth. As the action of Christ manifest in symbol, the washing is more than what it is on the merely physical level; insofar as it is symbolic activity, it is a bearer of salvation because it is a *sign*. It is only when we consider the physical aspect just in itself and then afterwards proceed to give it a higher significance that we unnecessarily complicate the relation between "sign" and "saving

44

causality". Because we are dealing with *sacramenta separata*, we can rightly call this symbolic causality an instrumental saving causality.

We should not forget, however, that this saving efficacy can be viewed in a twofold respect: as mystery of worship and as sanctification. In every sacrament, but especially in the Eucharist, both aspects operate *ex opere operato;* that means that in its sacramental manifestation the power of the redemptive grace of Christ operates *of itself*, both as prayerful *worship* and as efficacious *sanctification.* As sacramental mystery of worship, every sacrament, since it is supported by Christ and the whole community of the faithful in the Church, wins *ex opere operato* the sacramental grace for the one who is to receive it. This grace is then bestowed *ex opere operato* through the same sacrament as long as the man puts no obstacle in the way (i.e. if the adult recipient joins himself actively and religiously to the request included in this act of worship—a point which we will deal with in a moment). Precisely because of the efficacy of this act of worship or the sacramental value of the sacrament as prayer, as the sacramentalizing of the prayer of Christ in and through his Church, a valid sacrament that was received unfruitfully can *subsequently* "revivify". Even when a sacrament is perhaps unfruitful at the moment of reception, still, in a certain respect, no sacrament is *completely* unfruitful because of its value as a sacramental prayer of Christ and his entire Church.

The Sacrament as religious experience

The inner religious condition of the receiving subject is not merely a disposition which precedes or parallels the sacrament; it enters into the very essence of the fruitful sacrament. Of course, the religious experience contributes in no respect to the *validity* of the sacrament. Christ's demonstration of love has absolute priority over every human response and does not depend on it; rather, this response is supported by Christ's love. However, it remains true that only when some inchoate religious ardour is present in the believer who is to receive the sacrament will his sharing in the mystery of worship of the Church be a worthy sacramental expression of his inner spirit. Then this worthily received sacrament will become not only the worshipping petition of Christ and his Church but also that of the receiver: the sacramental expression of his religious desire for grace and his will to encounter Christ. If such a religious desire for encounter does not exist, the valid sacrament (i.e. Christ's will for encounter in and through his Church) cannot develop into a real mutual encounter. As a personal encounter with the glorified *Kyrios*, the sacrament which is completely genuine, therefore, necessarily implies the religious ardour of the receiving subject.

The personal religious dispositions of the receiver (which differ depending on whether we are dealing with a sacrament of the living or of the dead) will, therefore, be sacramentalized *in* the worshipping activity of the Church, which, then—solely by virtue of the redemption of Christ—bestows sacramental grace *ex opere operato*, that is, brings about the actual encounter with Christ. From this we see that the sacraments do not work automatically, but rather that, as a result of faith and a deep religious longing, they lay hold of the sanctifying power of Christ which is at work in the sacramental Church. But this grasping of salvation in faith is actually the person's *being grasped* by the redeeming Christ. ("The passion of Christ obtains its effect in those to whom it is applied through *faith and charity* and through the *sacraments of faith*."[9])

The sacraments are, therefore, no easier path to holiness, as though they could dispense us from a part of that religious striving which is demanded in order to attain the grace of reconciliation or interior intimacy with God outside the sacraments. As we have seen, the significance of sacraments as incarnations of the religious disposition is rather that they bring about *moments of supreme ardour* in the everyday Christian life. In contrast to the extrasacramental communion with God, the sacramental life of grace and love is the full and mature stature of the Christian life. As modern anthropology points out, there are in human life, besides the *decisive* or *momentous* actions in which the person achieves more intensive self-expression, also *everyday* actions in which personal freedom expresses itself in a lesser or more moderate degree. So also there are decisive Christian acts and also everyday acts of grace. Because of their sacramental incarnation, the sacramental acts of worship are intended to be decisive and momentous actions of the Christian life. They demand, therefore, more intensive deliberation and reflection; otherwise they become flat and are reduced to a soulless formalism. On the part of Christ too, the sacraments, as earthly embodiment of his heavenly saving act, are the tangible and complete intervention of his gracious will. Therefore, what is normally experienced as something *ordinary* outside the sacraments should grow in and through the sacraments toward a special crowning experience, toward full and complete maturity.

Thus, the seven sacraments indicate the high points of our Christian existence (*Dasein*). They give sharp and clear dimensions to everyday Christian life, which at regular intervals raise up the level of everyday spiritual life to new heights. In them the ordinary day-to-day pattern must once again be left behind and surpassed if it is not to fade into that colourless anonymity which, once sacramental practice is abandoned, leads in time to the surrender of Christianity itself and, finally, of all religious spirit.

The sacraments are God's own saving act as it manifests itself in the sacred realm of the Church, as it concretely addresses man and takes hold of him as perceptibly and visibly as a mother embraces her child. Although the child already realizes that his mother loves him, still this felt embrace gives the experience of love in its fullness. "Now we truly know." On our way to Emmaus which leads to the

Eschaton, the sacrament is the veiled encounter in which our heart, listening with eager and ardent faith, burns within us. "Did not our hearts burn within us while he talked to us on the road?" (Lk 24:32). Precisely because of their sacramental character, i.e. because the sacraments are an authentic, visible proof of Christ's desire to give grace to the one who receives them, they give us a tranquil, moral certitude of the reality of this gift of grace—a certitude which is lacking in grace bestowed outside the sacraments. This very fact makes us experience the divine graciousness of redemption even more intensely than the bestowal of grace outside the sacraments.

Analytical definition of the sacraments of the Church

On account of the different levels and the numerous factors which we discovered in the sacramental order of the Church, it is impossible to put together into a single sentence all the elements which go to make up a sacrament. The definition which has become classical, *signum efficax gratiae* (an efficacious sign of grace), is only a schematic cross-section of the abundant riches contained in the notion of sacrament. In concluding, we can now attempt to give a descriptive definition which progressively indicates the different essential elements of a sacrament.

A sacrament of the Church is (1) a personal saving act of the glorified Christ, an act of worship as well as sanctification—(2) in and through his Church which, in virtue of the authority and the sacramental character given to her by Christ, *sacramentalizes* this invisible act of the glorified Christ in a sanctifying mystery of worship of the Church. In this way, the once-for-all, eternally-actual redeeming act of the God-man is given a public, historically situated visibility on earth which renders it present among us and for us, and which is at the same time the manifestation of the Church's holy participation in it. The Church does this through the medium of its authorized minister who, therefore, must have the intention of "doing what the Church does". This intention is necessary to authentically sacramentalize the celestial saving act of Christ. What is essential to this early sacramentalizing is the ritual action of the Church in liturgical unity with the sacramental word of the Church. The symbolic signs and actions are borrowed from ordinary human life and, for the most part, they are things which already had a sacred meaning for religious man (ritual washing, anointing, imposition of hands, sacred meal, etc.). But through the word, this basic symbolism is caught up in the higher vision of the Church and thus elevated to the specific sacramental symbolism of the Church. In this ordinary *matter* supplied by man, which of itself is lifeless and impotent, Christ accomplishes in his Church, by the power of his salvific *word*, a deeper, divine mystery of salvation.

(3) This sanctifying act of worship of the glorified high priest in heaven, sacramentalized in and through the Church, is *directed essentially* to that particular

50

man in whom the sacrament is performed (consideration being made for the unique character of the
Eucharist as sacrifice of the Church and for the entire
Church). This is so completely true that this personal
involvement is part of the very essence of the sacrament; for this reason, the intention of the person to
receive a sacrament also contributes toward deter-
mining the validity or authentic sacramentalizing (i.e.
the making visible in an earthly way in the ministry
of the Church) of Christ's will to sanctify this person.
These first three elements are what constitute a *valid*
sacrament.

(4) However, this sanctifying sacramental mystery
of worship of Christ in and through his Church can
only develop *ex opere operato* all the rich fecundity
for which it was established when the subject for
whom the sacrament is intended also actively enters
with a religious spirit into this mystery of worship
with faith and an earnest longing for grace. Thus it
will also become the sacramental expression of his
personal desire to encounter Christ in faith.

This vital religious participation by the (adult)
recipient in the sacramental mystery of worship—a
participation which is itself already the fruit of grace
—now grows, through the saving efficacy of the
sacramental celebration, toward a more interior,
personal communion with Christ, toward a deeper
bond with the Church's community of grace, and,
therefore, to an increased intimacy of grace with the
living God: with the Father, the Son, and the Holy
Spirit.

From all of this it becomes quite clear that the sacraments are neither "things" nor "automatons" but rather, by virtue of genuine incarnation, a mutual personal involvement on the part of Christ and his Church (through the medium of its authorized minister) and also on the part of the believer who receives him, and who in his longing for grace lays hold of the living power of Christ which alone sanctifies and which is actively present in the Church. He does this through his reception in faith or, more correctly, through the *active part* he also plays *in the celebration* of the sacrament. The one same objective reality appearing in veiled sacral symbolic actions, namely, the sanctifying sacramental mystery of worship, thus becomes the expression of both the condescending *agape* (charity) of God and of the longing of the man of faith who strives to reach above and beyond himself. In the liturgical, sacramental mystery of worship the theophany of the redeeming God is accomplished and man succeeds in returning home to the Father in Christ through the Spirit of sanctification. "You have showed yourself to me face to face. O Christ; it is you that I find in your sacraments.[10]"

2. Marriage in the Divine Revelation of the Old Testament

"As God of old made himself present to his people through a covenant of love and fidelity, so now the Saviour of men and the Spouse of the Church comes into the lives of married Christians through the sacrament of matrimony. . . . Authentic married love is caught up into divine love and is governed and enriched by Christ's redeeming power and the saving activity of the Church."—*Pastoral Constitution on the Church in the Modern World*, II, 1, 48.

The Old Testament and the Christian understanding of marriage

The Old Testament merits a place of special honour in any consideration of the saving reality of marriage. Of course, it is true that it is only when seen from the point of view of the complete revelation of Christ that marriage can be perceived in its full light. Nonetheless, one of the most important elements which Christianity has inherited from Israel is the Old Testament's living, almost passionate, and certainly joyous confession of everyday secular values, understood not as self-contained, but as dynamic and proceeding directly from God. The vision which we derive from the Old Testament comes as an intense relief, especially in an age of closed secularization in marriage as well as in most other spheres. It is in the Old Testament more than anywhere else that we can come into immediate contact with the concrete experience of the goodness of secular values and realities. These are never allowed to evaporate—to become insubstantial, supernatural, and falsely mystical qualities. Nor are they ever held in contempt. In the Old Testament they are always recognized and lived as something matter-of-fact and belonging to this world. Yet this very "worldliness" was for Israel a divine miracle—the "work of his hands" and a source of grace for man.

Since marriage is first and foremost a secular value, and since it entered salvation history as a secular reality, we may reasonably expect Israel to have a great deal to impart to us as Christians, perhaps of a cautionary nature. It may well be that Israel, as the people of God, can help us not only to avoid placing too much emphasis on the sacramental aspect of this secular, anthropological reality, but also to avoid the error of underestimating this aspect of marriage. It is precisely this vision of the people of God which Christianity should strive to preserve and illuminate in the light of Christ.

Our search is for the word of God concerning marriage, the word which has been heard with a gradually increasing clarity throughout salvation history and which, at this moment of time, claims our attention with particular authority. In the first place this means that we must seek to answer the question: How did Israel, as the people of God, experience the reality of marriage? I stress, *Israel as the people of God*, since it is frequently forgotten that everything that is "biblical"—that is to say, everything that is to be found in the Bible—is not necessarily the word of revelation, even though it is inspired. Expressions such as "biblical anthropology" or the "biblical relationship between man and woman" have a double meaning. They may just denote, quite straightforwardly, the ancient oriental, and more particularly the Semitic, view of man or of marriage; in which case, the dogmatic question as to what is "biblical" in the Old Testament in the theological sense of the word—that is, as the expression of God's word which is binding on Christians—remains unanswered. Sometimes it is simply a matter of the concrete framework, determined by the historical period and the social environment in which it is set, within which the word of God comes to us. To overlook this important distinction, especially in connection with marriage, may well result in letting loose the forces of reaction—with regard, for example, to modern views on marriage and the family which are set in a different social and historical framework, but which are nonetheless reconcilable with God's word.

On the other hand, the fact remains that it pleased God to reveal himself within a Semitic society and in the course of a Semitic history, and from the dogmatic point of view this must always be seen as a caution to us. We can ignore this history and civilization only at our peril, for it is impossible to grasp the word of God as a pure, divine reality somehow divorced from its human expression. It is precisely in Israelite man that the Old Testament revelation comes to us. For this reason the Israelite expression of God's word is not in itself determined by the historical and social setting, but is rather formed by its being at the service of God's revelation. The form of expression and what is expressed are, of course, different, but they cannot be separated like the pieces of two puzzles and then put together to build up two distinct pictures. Many aspects of Israel's social and historical setting bear the imprint of divine revelation or of her association with the living God. Many voices, not always in harmony with each other, have warned against the danger of divorcing God's word from Israel, since, by so doing, we cannot guarantee that we shall in fact hear God's meaning more clearly.

It is remarkable how Christians of today, living, as they believe, in an age of biblical renewal, seem to listen less seriously and less obediently than in "unbiblical" times to God's Word concerning marriage. Indeed, they appear to confine their interest solely to man's experience of his own existence. But in my opinion this self-interpretation, this examination of our own human experience, only deserves to be called truly biblical and Christian when it is conducted in the light of the revelation of God's Word. It is only when we repeatedly measure our own experience of our human existence—which always contains, albeit anonymously, the element of factual revelation—against God's word concerning man and at the same time concerning himself that we really begin to practise authentic theology.

Salvation history as a marriage drama and marriage as a prophetic figure

The Old Testament view saw marriage fundamentally as a secular reality and therefore as a good gift of God. But Yahweh was a God of salvation. Both in its aspect of specifically human and personal relation-

58

ships between man and wife and its family aspect, marriage in Israel entered the history of salvation which was directed towards Christ. Both marriage and the family thus had the function of serving the plan of salvation which led to Christ.

The use of marriage as an image of the community life of Israel with Yahweh is rich in theological content. It is, however, important to remember that this is only one of many images used in the Old Testament to express the same relationship between God and man. Among these are the father-and-son relationship, the king-and-subject relationship (the image of the kingdom of God), and the lord or master and servant or slave relationship.[11] In the master and servant relationship, it is the inequality of the partners which strikes us, an inequality which, although certainly present in Israelitic marriage, is never emphasized in the Old Testament marriage image when this is used to express the communion of God with his people. In the context of the covenant at least, married love and fidelity pointed above all to a communion or dialogue between two partners. The subordinate position of the wife was never particularly stressed, apart from the fact that the husband, Yahweh, always took the initiative, and —in his sovereign freedom—overwhelmed his chosen bride with gifts. In any case, the marriage image was more suitable than the other images used in the Old Testament for the purpose of expressing the religious interpersonal relationship, the direct and intimate dialogue, between God and his people, who were

59

God's "beloved". The various images were thus complementary to each other.

Moreover, one striking feature of the use of the symbolism of marriage for the covenant of grace is that it coincided with the emergence for the first time of a clear theology of the history of salvation in the eighth century B.C. The image of marriage, a secular, human, and changing reality, pointed less to the covenant as such than to the dialectic of the covenant of grace—to the concrete historicity of life in communion with Yahweh, the God of history. The dynamic and indeed dramatic course of man's relationship with God, and of God's sovereign and free saving activity with man, was clearly illuminated in the marriage image. This image was used especially for the purpose of expressing this concrete historical truth. Hosea, Jeremiah, Ezekiel, and Deutero-Isaiah, all of whom used this image, saw the course of Israel's history as a tortuous, but none the less continuous, line with a beginning, a middle, and, in the future, an end.

The beginning was situated in the early period of love, the time of the betrothal and the wedding which followed it. Hosea (2:17), Jeremiah (2:2), and Ezekiel (23:3, 8, 19, 21) each placed his own individual emphasis on this phase, but each set it in the period between the deliverance from Egypt and the entry into the promised land, that is, during the sojourn in the desert. (The tradition of the murmuring of the people of God in the desert was apparently not known to these prophets, although of course

60

Ezekiel toned down the idealistic picture of this time of early love and recognized in it an hereditary taint.)

This, then, was the time of God's and Israel's youthful love for each other, their honeymoon—the time when Israel's "whoredom" with Egypt was no longer possible, and her "whoredom" with the Baal of Canaan not yet possible. According to these prophets, God did in fact make it impossible for Israel to be unfaithful to him, Yahweh, by committing adultery, and this shows that they sensed Israel's inherent weakness as Yahweh's spouse. It was only when Yahweh placed Israel in a historical situation where it was impossible for her to be guilty of "whoredom" that everything went well. (There was in this, too, an element of the corrective punishment which Yahweh was to impose upon faithless Israel.)

Israel's marriage in the desert is thus the point of reference from which the later course of the nation's life should be viewed. The patriarchal period, the sojourn in Egypt, and the Exodus were (we may say) the birth, the youth, and the "marriageable age" of the people of God. Israel's day-to-day married life, with all its ups and downs, began from the time that the nation settled in Canaan. The trust in himself which Yahweh demanded of Israel when he led her through the desert, and which Israel herself, according to this tradition, placed without reserve in him at that time, should have been the norm for Israel's married life with God. The past—the wedding— was the model for the further course of their life together. It was in Yahweh, and in no one else, that

Israel was to place her hope and trust. From this point of reference Israel's present life was judged to be adultery and infidelity, committed in spite of Yahweh's constant love for her, a love which penetrated to her very heart. This opened up a perspective into the future, a perspective of either salvation or disaster. If Israel were to seek help and protection from others, let her do so—but in that case she would discover that, if Yahweh was "not a God" for her, she would eventually be ruined, helpless, and reviled. Infidelity in response to Yahweh's love would bring its own punishment. On the other hand, if she returned to Yahweh—and this was only possible because he never regarded her leaving him as a permanent divorce—he would prove to her that all good gifts, including profane ones, were dependent upon him and upon him alone.

What is remarkable, in any consideration of the present and the future of Israel's life, is that the marriage covenant between Yahweh and Israel was placed "in the background"—that it was situated in the past as a milestone, a firm, unshakable reality established once and for all time. For the present and the future the image of children was used more than that of two partners in marriage. Israel of the present was, of course, the fruit of Yahweh's and Israel's marital love for each other in the desert, and the present stage of Yahweh's and Israel's relationship with each other was concerned with the children of that love. Love itself was the *prōton*, the constitutive initial phase, of the relationship, existing at the very

62

beginning as an unassailable, constant, and indissoluble reality. The infidelity and defection took place in the "children of Israel", for Israel was a mother who bore faithless and renegade children (Hos 2:4, 6, 7). The ultimate vision, then, also points to the return of Israel's children (Is 49:20–21; 54:1). And so there was no question of a permanent divorce, only of a temporary separation, and this was not because in the last resort Israel's dispositions were basically good, but because Yahweh was eternal and unshakable in his love. Hosea and the other prophets saw the course of salvation history as above all a "happy ending", with the exception of Ezekiel, who in chapter 23 merely allows the final result to be guessed at—the two wives Judah and Israel, the one people of God, were "stoned to death" according to the law for their divorce from Yahweh. It is precisely when the covenant of grace is understood as a marriage between Yahweh and Israel that this flexible, far-reaching vision is possible, for Israel is essentially a *historical* quantity. On the other hand, it is precisely this marriage-image which implies that Yahweh personally participated in Israel's history. The changeable nature of marriage is therefore the best available vehicle for conveying as a message the dialectic of the history of salvation and of disaster.

It is also remarkable that the first time (as far as we know) that the marriage-image was used in the Old Testament to express God's love for Israel, the purely allegorical aspect was transcended—a concrete, secular marriage between two Israelites, Hosea and Gomer, became the prophetic symbol of the historical love-dialogue between God and his people. Even where the book of Ezekiel describes the concrete history of Israel's salvation and disaster in her relationship with God allegorically as a marriage, it is more than mere allegory. It is an image pointing to a reality which for men could hardly be expressed differently, but which is every bit as real as the vicissitudes of married life. Moreover, the image is more remarkable still, in that—in Ezekiel—it implies too an ethical message for the concrete married life of the Israelites. If the Old Testament is read first of all on its own, and then afterwards in the light of the New Testament and of the later history of the Church, it is impossible not to sense that the Old Testament was already aware of an intimate relationship between concrete human marriage on the one hand and, on the other, true piety or the relationship of man with God—that concrete marriage in the Old Testament has a certain "sacramental" quality. Moreover, this realisation is a universal fact in religious mankind.

But in this connection we must be careful to bear in mind that the full light of the Old Testament revelation could only come to bear on this reality when it had first inculcated the idea of the one God, the absolute transcendence of the God who was above sexuality. The sacramental quality of marriage could not become visible in its purest form until the reality of marriage was first seen as a secular, creaturely reality, stripped of all myths and rites

64

referring to a "non-God"—or (more accurately) to the one, true God whom men had so misrepresented and so fashioned according to their own image that it was difficult for them to conceive and to experience marriage "in God's image". For this reason the Old Testament had first to strip marriage of all its pagan religious connotations. In this way it is possible to see in the Song of Solomon, as it first appeared and was understood in Israel, the culminating point of the process of demythologization of human erotic love and sexuality. It is then possible to see the same Song—in its later Jewish, and still later Christian, re-reading and interpretation—as the culminating point of man's attempt to express the inexpressible dialogue of love between God and his people, the Church that he was to adorn as his bride and make permanently his own. But this prophetic allegorical usage was more than an image leaving marriage as something purely secular. Marriage, precisely as marriage, would of itself appear to have a prophetic form.

3. Revelation, Scripture, Tradition, and Teaching Authority

"Sacred tradition and sacred Scripture form one sacred deposit of the Word of God, which is committed to the Church. . . . The task of authentically interpreting the Word of God, whether written or handed on, has been entrusted exclusively to the living teaching office of the Church, whose authority is exercised in the name of Jesus Christ."—*Dogmatic Constitution on Divine Revelation*, II, 10.

Although it is possible to speak of an anonymous revelation outside the Jewish–Christian religion only in the light of the historical reality which is Christ, and in no other way, I propose to postulate, at least for the sake of this enquiry, which aims at being a synthesis, this anonymous revelation. What is in fact an implication or a consequence of Christianity will be seen here as its general background. It is necessary to state this explicitly at the outset, in order to avoid giving the impression that this preliminary consideration is unbiblical. What I have to say here will moreover be set out schematically, since I aim to do no more than provide a basis for discussion between Catholic and Protestant theologians.

The background to and the "heart" of Christian revelation: God's effective saving will

We know, through the divine revelation in Christ, that God intended that all men should be saved in Christ and, what is more, that this salvation not only was a possibility in Christ, but also has actually been brought by Christ, for all men, even though who in fact attains this salvation remains a mystery for us.

That is why it is possible to say that wherever men make history, a history of salvation or of perdition is brought about, because the significance they give their life is always, in acceptance or refusal, a response to the anonymous grace of God, his call to salvation. History is essentially a history made by human freedom. The real place where the human world becomes history is human freedom. If this freedom is confronted with Christ's salvation, though perhaps anonymously, in the universal and effective saving will of God, then this (implicit) confrontation with God's universal will to save—universal because it is concrete and individual with regard to *all* men— *de facto* causes a history of salvation or of perdition. Seen in the perspective of grace, secular human history is, via human freedom which responds in a negative or a positive way (and which makes history), a history of salvation or of perdition. On the other hand, however, the freedom of the individual entering this world and its already formed human history also encounters an already existing history of salvation or of perdition, with the result that history itself has something to tell him, as it were from outside, about the God of salvation.

Included in the perspective of salvation from which God's attentive concern appeals to man through grace, man's situation is also characterized by the dynamic element of this call to salvation. The world, which was offered by God to man so that it should be given human significance, was offered to him concretely by the God of salvation. Thus, within the interior attraction of grace in which God offers the grace of faith to man, the world of creation, which is above all the world of one's fellow men, is a reference not only to the creative God, but also in the concrete sense to the living God, the God of salvation. In this way, creation, secular history, and man's encounter with his fellow men are all brought within the orbit of salvation. Within God's universally effective will to save, the world, as creation, as human history, and as human encounter acquires a special significance which it would not otherwise have of its own accord; it appears to us at the same time as a translation, however inadequate, of God's inward appeal to us through grace, as a means in and through which man is made more explicitly aware of this inward offer of grace, and finally as a sphere within which man may respond, either positively or negatively, to this divine appeal. That is why it is possible for us to say that, at least in the perspective of the saving mystery of Christ, the history of salvation or of perdition is as extensive as the human world itself. In other words, the history of salvation is not restricted exclusively to the religion of Israel or to Christianity, but is, because of Christ, an event of universal significance.

It is, however, also possible to dispute the extent to which we may speak of an authentic revelation in this connection outside the sphere of public revelation. In itself, God's inward appeal to us through grace may only be called revelation in its outward manifestation, for it always comes to us from outside—"from what is heard" (Rom 10:17). Outside Israel and Christianity there is an anonymous, and therefore vague and ambiguous, though undoubtedly existent, *auditus exterior* ("hearing from outside"): the world of creation as the translation of God's inward communication to man. The whole of secular human life thus somehow makes explicit what God's inward offer of grace means for us, namely, that God is our salvation. What is brought about in the secular world is the same as what is brought about in the concrete appearance of the same saving will of God, that is, in the man Jesus, with the difference that the first is vague, ambiguous, easy to misinterpret and therefore frequently misinterpreted, whereas the second cannot be misunderstood. Only Christ is the absolutely clear saving will of God. Although a presentiment of this saving will was felt outside Israel and christianity (in grace), its true aspect was only seen in Christ. That is why we refer to a revelation in the whole of human history, a revelation which is truly supernatural but anonymous, and indeed to the anonymous revelation of Christ himself, incomplete and therefore open to misinterpretation. This is not an *a priori* deduction, but the implication of a twofold (Catholic) Christian truth that the possibility of salvation exists (in Christ) for all men, even if they are historically and concretely not confronted with Christianity, and that salvation is impossible without faith (see Heb 11:6). Faith is man's surrender to divine revelation. On a basis, then, of the absolute necessity of faith for salvation, God's universal will to save includes the real possibility that all men, wherever they live, may accept salvation by (anonymous) faith, and thus be anonymously confronted with God's saving revelation. In other words: "In past generations he allowed all the nations to walk in their own ways; *yet* he did not leave himself without witness, for he did good . . ." (Acts 14:16–17). This was said of the concrete and living God.

The history of salvation and the prophetic message

1. *In Israel.* Against the background and in the climate of this universal, anonymous invitation to communion with the living God, God began to clarify, as it were in an official manner, the meaning of his saving will, and he did this in Israel. Although we must always take care to assess the phenomenon of Israel as something which is distinct and independent from the religions of the ancient Near East, we must at the same time not use this as a reason for denying all continuity between Israel and the surrounding, anonymously supernatural religions. Anonymous revelation became in Israel a particular, concrete and "public" revelation, deriving the elements through which it found expression from the religious manifestations of "universal revelation". Judgement was at the same time pronounced by the particular revelation of Israel on the non-Israelitic religions, in which human religious consciousness had

73

tried to give a concrete but ambiguous form to universal revelation.

Israel's history of salvation is distinguished from the universal history of salvation by the presence of the prophetic message in Israel's history. The word of God which, speaking, makes the history of salvation, became, via the prophets of Israel, a word that interpreted Israel's history at its saving value. By virtue of the critical function of Israel's prophets, who spoke in the name of the God of salvation but also had their roots in Israel's faith, this word brought divine revelation into the history of Israel in an unambiguous manner. It is therefore in the revelation of the word that the formal distinction between Israel's particular and "public" revelation and universal and anonymous revelation is to be found.

That this divine word was heard in Israel and not elsewhere points moreover to a particular election of this people with Christ in view. It is not that the "covenant" as such, the intersubjective relationship of a people with its God, was peculiar to Israel. The religions of Israel's neighbours were also familiar with a kind of "covenant" with their God—it was the will of the living God that all should be saved, and Israel herself was aware that she had not been chosen because of her own merits. Many of the Old Testament prophets recognised that God could have called another pagan people. But the fact that the revelation of the word occurred precisely in Israel points to God's particular concern with the history

74

of this people. Although Israel did not become conscious of the universal saving significance of her election as a mediation for all men until late in her history, the history of her salvation was nonetheless— seen in the perspective of Christ—a veiled pre-revelation of the mystery of Christ. This is so precisely because the history of salvation was "accompanied" in Israel by the message of the prophets, in which salvation became transparent. God's saving activity became visible and tangible as acts of God in history because of the word, and always with Christ in view.

Thus, although revelation is fundamentally situated in Yahweh's activity for the salvation of his people, and therefore in the history of Israel, the saving value of this history was only interpreted by the prophetic message. Israel's saving history gained its full and clear meaning as revelation when Israel listened to the message of the prophets. God's saving activity is not only a divine action, but also a divine interpretation of this action, in and through the prophetic message. The secular event of Israel's exodus from Egypt thus has a real saving significance, and it does not have this only in the theological reflection of the pious. As a secular historical event the exodus itself is a saving act of God, a revelation of salvation. But this saving act only becomes de facto an aspect of *our* history, i.e. a part of our consciousness and reflection, in and through the word. Yahweh said to Moses: "I have seen the affliction of my people who are in Egypt, and have heard their cry because of their taskmasters; . . . I have come down to deliver them (Ex 3:7–8). It is in this word that God's saving act, accomplished in the historical fact itself, and his revelation of himself formally became for us revelation. God's saving activity—revelation in reality—and his word—revelation in word—are therefore indissolubly united to each other in the one concept of revelation. Both are essential ingredients of the one divine revelation.

It may be regarded as characteristic that the fundamental saving events of the Jewish people were marked by the appearance, whether before, during, or after these events, of a prophetic figure who interpreted Israel's national history in the light of her consciousness of faith, in which these prophets were themselves involved. The prophetic message threw light on the presence and the content of the saving act and, if the message preceded the events, even brought about the presence of a saving fact. It was precisely because salvation was revealed in a veiled manner in an event belonging strictly to this world, that is, in Jewish history, that the unerring recognition of the fact as a fact of salvation required the prophetic message. The word thus forms an integral part of the manifestation of God's saving activity. It is, of course, true that God did not simply say something about salvation. He also accomplished salvation within history. But, if this history was to be experienced as saving history, he had to interpret its meaning in and through the message of the prophets. The history of salvation, or God's saving activity as revelation, was for this reason an interpreted history, interpreted under a divine guarantee.

2. *In Christ.* If divine revelation has an essential bearing upon God's saving love for man, then this divine saving love for man in history of its very nature means promise and faithfulness. (See Deut 7:8–10.) The revelation-in-word therefore stands in the sign of the promise and its fulfilment, and man's temporal and spatial situation is the material with which God shows his love and invites man to respond to this love. As an event consisting essentially of dialogue between God and man, revelation, because of man's position in a world of fellow human beings and things in which he makes history, is of its very nature accomplished in history. It is therefore impossible to separate God's elective love from man's association with this world in which he makes history. The history of mankind's salvation, in the form in which this became clear for the first time in the history of Israel, was—seen in the perspective of the mystery of Christ—in Israel a problematic reality, since God did not speak his definitive word in Israel.

Israel's history merged into the coming of the Son of God into the history of our world. As an act of God in historical form, the whole of Jesus' human life was revelation. From his dialogue with the Father the Son entered our human history, which thereby became, because of Jesus' human freedom, definitive saving history. But the definitive entry of this salvation in Christ into our history can be historically recognized only in the prophetic message of the same Christ, and only by those who believe in this message. It is only through the revelation of Christ's word that the saving significance of the revelation-in-reality which has been accomplished in the life and death of Christ becomes accessible to us historically in faith. It is precisely because salvation offers itself to us as a supernatural reality in the form of an earthly, secular reality—the humanity of Christ— that this saving reality appears as given and as revealed to us in the word.[12] The manifestation of the historical appearance of salvation in Christ thus includes Christ's prophetic message as an essential element in its constitution.

The history of salvation, the word, and the sacred books

1. From her history of salvation and the word, there emerged in Israel a consciousness of salvation, a consciousness that it was God's special people. Throughout the course of its history, the nation became more and more deeply aware of its religious significance and of its being the people of God. In this way, living traditions developed in Israel, and these traditions, together with its history of salvation and the word, formed a single whole constituting Israel as the people of God. Israel, however, frequently interpreted its history wrongly, in an all too human way. The prophetic message therefore acted as a constant critical authority in Israel, sifting what was authentic in these traditions from what was not authentic.

The sacred books of Israel gradually emerged against this background of saving history and traditions, brought about or critically sifted by the message of the prophets, and it was in these books that Israel's consciousness of salvation was reflected via the critical interpretation of the prophets. These books appeared with the divine guarantee that this written expression of Israel's consciousness of salvation was a faithful reflection of the saving plan that God himself wished to realize in his people. The inspiration of these writings was therefore an extension of the divine and interpretative element expressed in the prophetic message, which in its turn was also supported by Israel's consciousness of salvation. In this sense, the inspiration of these books was, on the one hand, a personal charism, peculiar to the sacred writer himself. On the other hand, however, the sacred writer wrote precisely as a member of the people of God and in the service of this people. The inspired written word must therefore be seen, via the prophetic message, in association with Israel's history of salvation. The scriptural message thus had its roots deep in Israel's history: "What lay behind the whole of Israel's national life was the inspiration which proceeded from this mystery, and which gave form and shape to the great diversity of material resulting from historical events and the various statements of the people."[13]

2. A similar process occurred in the apostolic Church in connection with the salvation brought

about by the man Jesus. The saving event and the word of Christ, received, experienced, and heard by the apostolic Church, in which the idea developed among the early Christian community that it was the redeemed people of God and the Church of the Lord, eventually found their way, via the preaching and the witness of the apostles, into the Holy Scripture of the New Testament. On the one hand the hagiographers of the New Testament wrote as members of the Church which was being built up, but on the other the apostolic message and the literature of the New Testament were at the same time the interpretative element by means of which the saving significance of the mystery of Christ, as this was experienced in the early Church, was authentically proclaimed to the world under a divine guarantee.

Revelation-in-reality, revelation-in-word, and holy scripture thus form one single whole. Scripture provides us with an infallible and precise expression of the revelation as this was revealed in God's saving activity in Christ, in a veiled manner in Christ's prehistory in the Old Testament, and indeed even in the remote prehistory of the whole of mankind. Scripture is an essential element of the redeeming mystery of Christ as divine revelation.

The apostolic Church and its scripture as opposed to the post-apostolic Church

1. The apostolic Church read the Old Testament in the light of the event of Christ. In this sense, the books of the Old Testament belonged to the books of the Church of Christ. The Old Testament certainly had an independent significance of its own for Israel, but it was the beginning of a work, the last sentence of which was completed in the New Testament, and this final sentence elucidated the initial sentence. In this context, it is important to note that the Old Testament only discloses its full meaning when faced with the saving reality of Christ.[14] Many different biblical meanings in the Old Testament escape notice outside this contact with Christ. We should certainly not assume that the apostolic Church read things into the Old Testament that were not there. On the contrary, nothing more was read into the words than they in fact said. It is simply that the deepest meaning of the books of the Old Testament was discovered in the apostolic Church— a meaning which was only apparent to those who, in faith and because of the apostolic witness, were confronted with the reality of the mystery of Christ. The words of Holy Scripture therefore also have a value which transcends their meaning within their contemporary context, since Scripture must always be a message for the present time.

What Scripture has to tell us is the divinely guaranteed apostolic expression of the single and non-recurrent apostolic contact with the earthly and glorified reality of Christ. It was in the apostolic period, and only in this period, that redemption was definitively brought about, even though the eschatological manifestation of redemption did not end in the apostolic age. Revelation, too, was thus definitively brought about and in that sense closed. The history of salvation of course continued, but the definitive statement of God's plan with the whole of human history had been made. The public revelation-in-word closed with the completion of the great event of the resurrection of the dead Christ. A definitive interpretation of human history was thus provided in Scripture. We can expect no other judgement on history than the judgement passed on it by the death and resurrection of Christ and proclaimed in Scripture.

Clearly, then, the history of salvation that followed the event of Christ's resurrection had a different meaning from that which preceded this event. Revelation—definitively brought about, closed, and therefore brought to fullness—acted as a norm in the life of the Church. (This is of course the reason why the college of bishops, headed by the successor to St. Peter, did not assume all the rights of Peter and the apostles.) Scripture is the 'covering letter' accompanying the mystery of the redemption brought about by God in the man Jesus, and it is clear that God intended it to be the lasting document accompanying this definitive saving event. In its later life the whole of the Church, including the ecclesiastical

82

or hierarchical office of that Church, would have to refer to the apostolic Church with its scripture. The apostolic Church is the canon of the Church's faith, the norm of the whole of the Church's life, and consequently Scripture is also the canon and norm of the Church's life of faith because of its apostolic character. The apostolic Church together with its scripture is therefore the *norma non normanda*—the norm in its own right—of the whole of the post-apostolic Church. Since Scripture belongs to the phase in the history of salvation in which the apostolic tradition was constituted, it is, as the written tradition of the college of apostles, the Magna Carta against which the life and the confession of the Church must always be verified.

2. On the other hand, however, it is not possible to give an independent value to this "covering letter", as if salvation were to be found exclusively in Scripture. It is generally the case that truth is not to be found above all and formally—I say explicitly, *formally*—in a book, but in the consciousness of a living human community, insofar as this community is directed towards reality, which ultimately is the truth. This is also the case in regard to religious truth. Saving truth is the meaningful content of the life of faith of the entire Church, which recognizes itself in Scripture. The living reality is always richer than the written expression of this reality, at least as far as its literal and explicit meaning is concerned. But this written expression in itself contains a dynamism

which embraces an inner reference to the fullness of the saving truth. Scripture is, after all, the word of God in human form. The divine Word, thus given human form, transcends the directly analysable sense of these human words, which thus go beyond their purely human meaning and refer objectively beyond themselves: this is the *sensus plenior* of Scripture, that is, the deepest meaning of the word of God, which is only very gradually made fully explicit within the life of the Church.

The revelation-in-word is directed, through the medium of the history of salvation and therefore through the medium of Scripture as well, to the whole of humanity, and inwardly to the heart of each individual, including ourselves, who live in the Church today. This means that Scripture has, so to speak, a double context: its context within the apostolic Church, and its present-day context. For Scripture is the record and the fundamental, divinely guaranteed expression of our present-day faith as well. Thus through the centuries the Church, constantly deriving its life and faith from the Bible, has always been in process of reclaiming the more implicit meaning of Scripture, on a basis of the grace of faith which empowers us to be "sympathetic" to the divine meaning of the Bible's human words. This development has never resulted, and will never result, in the discovery of any new dogmas or revelations: any such we should have to find elsewhere than in Scripture, as though the apostles had ignored the Bible and confided some truths of faith

84

to us in secret. The apostolic tradition which grew into Scripture will always be the expression constituting the apostles' own, and thus our own, consciousness of faith, though this can never be adequately put into words or into writing.

This consciousness of faith, which, through the grace of faith, is based on the totality of revelation, leads to a deeper understanding of the divine meaning of the human, scriptural word in direct proportion to the extent to which the Church lives in history in the light of the explicit statement of the Bible, in faithful contact with the saving reality itself. In this sense, the life of Christianity does not depend exclusively on the *sola scriptura*. Christ does not confront us exclusively with the sacred books, addressing us at the same time, inwardly and personally, through the testimony of his Spirit in accordance with the inclination of the grace of faith. We are also made citizens of the kingdom of God and members of Christ's body in the "sacrament of faith", called by Gregory of Nyssa the "first *traditio*". It is clear, then, that the concept *traditio non scripta*, as opposed to holy scripture, is wrongly translated as "oral tradition". This translation is one-sided and incomplete, since it is not primarily a question of an "oral" but of an "unwritten" tradition, and this is first and foremost the handing on of the saving reality itself, through which the Christian comes into contact not just with the apostolic Word but with the saving reality which is indicated by the Word and can only be experienced reflectively in the power of the Word.

85

The celebration of the mystery of the Eucharist, the Christian's prayerful contact with the reality of salvation, and his reception into the living charity of the Christian community all form part of the so-called "unwritten" traditions.

What has been handed down to us, for example, in connection with the Eucharist, is not simply the scriptural account or a doctrine about the eucharistic mystery, but the reality itself of the Eucharist. And it is in contact with this reality that Christians are able to come to a deeper understanding of the meaning of the Eucharist and to explicate it more fully.

A comparison may help to make this clearer. In the earliest Church, the Gospel of St. Matthew, read and interpreted in the light of apostolic experience and of association with the mystery of Christ, disclosed the content of this saving mystery by an appeal to the Old Testament, which yielded its deepest mystery in contact with the living and definitive reality of salvation. In the same way, involvement in the saving reality of the glorified Lord living in the Church is the only sphere in which the inner meaning of the New Testament can be fully understood. Our association with the reality of salvation is always differently situated in accordance with our changing circumstances. "Alongside" scripture, but never independent of it, we must therefore distinguish an element that, as such, cannot be traced back to the scriptural element. This is our living involvement in the saving reality itself, in the charity of the Christian

86

community, in the worship of the Church, in prayer, and so on.

It is true that this living contact is only brought about in faith, and thus when we believe in God's word and in scripture. But this does not mean that there is only contact with Christ in the word. There is in fact a contact in reality, although this only becomes explicitly conscious in belief in the word. Here too, revelation-in-reality and revelation-in-word are indissolubly united, and a denial of the validity of one of these elements makes the other meaningless. The inexhaustible meaning of Scripture has always been, and will continue to be, more fully disclosed in the experiential knowledge of the Church throughout the centuries in contact with the saving reality itself, of which the scriptures form an essential part. This does not imply that our association with the saving reality results in our reading more into Scripture than the words themselves say. It does, however, mean that, in our contact with the saving mystery, the inner significance of the "covering letter" is bound to emerge with greater and greater clarity. This saving mystery is itself the *sensus plenior* of Scripture, the "fuller meaning" of which is precisely the saving reality which is indicated in the human words.

There is, however, a difference between the reading and reinterpretation of the Old Testament in the light of living contact with Christ, as occurred in the case of the sacred writers of the New Testament, and our reading and interpretation of the Old and

New Testaments in the light of our communion-in-faith with the Lord who is present in the Church. The New Testament is the "covering letter" of salvation that has been definitively completed. The possibility of being able to reinterpret this Scripture from the point of view of a new phase of salvation is of its own nature excluded, since salvation in Christ is a definitive reality that will never be surpassed. (It is only the eschatological revelation that will go beyond Scripture and render it superfluous.) Our association with the saving reality is therefore a communion with the glorified Lord, to whom the scriptures bear witness. That is why the *ephapax*, the unique event of the mystery of Christ, and the apostolic testimony of this event in Scripture always act as a norm to the conscious content of our knowledge through contact with the saving reality.

Tradition in the Church, which, according to the Council of Trent, should be treated with "equal reverence" as Scripture, is an apostolic, and therefore a biblical, tradition. It is, in other words, the *paradosis* itself of the apostles. But this *paradosis* is a handing on both of realities of salvation, such as the celebration of the Eucharist, and of the message which grew into Scripture. The whole of the Church is thus, even in its teaching office, first and foremost an *ecclesia discens*, a learning Church, with regard to what is revealed, before it becomes in its magisterium an *ecclesia docens*, a teaching Church, for us. Ignatius of Antioch was acutely aware of this when he wrote that

88

the Church had constantly to seek refuge in the scriptures "as in the body of the Lord". And in the words of Augustine, which were repeated again and again through the Middle Ages, "everything that we need for our life of faith and our moral life can be found in what is stated explicitly in Scripture."[15]

The whole of the Church's life, in other words, ecclesiastical tradition, must refer at all times to the apostolic Church with its scriptures as to its norm, if it is to remain pure in its living growth, if it is to be revived and even if its theological expression is to be reformed and its perhaps one-sided religious experience is to be reorientated. In this connection, reformed Christianity, drawing its sustenance from the explicit testimony of the Bible, is a constant admonition to us Catholics, and often a legitimate protest.

Scripture and tradition in the context of the ecclesiastical office

Revelation in word and deed is not handed down within the Church in a mechanical way, like a dead thing passed on from hand to hand. It is, on the contrary, essentially linked with its living subject, the Church, consisting of the living people of God headed by the ecclesiastical office, both of which are under the guidance of the Spirit of the heavenly Lord. The entire Church is subject to tradition—the Church which prays and lives in faith, hope, and love, the Church which celebrates the liturgical mysteries, the Church which is apostolically effective in its office and in its people, and the Church which reflects on its faith. The entire Church carries out this tradition, but each part of the Church does this in its own place and in its own way, the laity as the people of God and the office of the Church in its hierarchical leadership. In addition, the ecclesiastical office as a whole also has a critical function.

Everything that comes about and is brought to light within the life of the Church must be carefully considered according to its apostolic and biblical content. It is true that this consideration is also the task of everyone in the Church, both laypeople and those holding office, but it is the exclusive function of the teaching office of the Church finally to judge whether we are faced, in connection with any definite reaction on the part of the people of the Church, with an infallible, apostolic, and biblical reaction, or with a human—and perhaps all too human—reaction. In this sense, the Church's teaching office is the judge of our faith, but it is this because it is itself governed by the norm of Scripture. The magisterium of the Church does not, therefore, stand above Scripture, but it does stand above our interpretation of Scripture. According to the Catholic view, then, Scripture has a critical function with regard to the concrete and empirical appearance of the Church. It is fundamentally Christ himself who interprets Scripture through his Spirit, active in the entire Church and in a special way in the office of the Church.

The infallibility of the Church's faith—an infallibility in which the Church's faith, the charism of the college of bishops, and the official charism of the pope as the head of this college form an indissoluble unity—is based upon the *ephapax*, the definitive character of the Christian mystery of salvation with its accompanying document, Scripture, beyond which we can never go. In other words, this infallibility has an eschatological basis: "The word of the Lord abides for ever. That word is the good news which was preached to you [in the gospel]" (1 Pet 1:25; see also Is 40:8). The word of God abides for ever in Christ, the *eschaton:* "I am sure that Christ is able to guard until that Day what has been entrusted to me" (2 Tim 1:12); "and when the Spirit of truth comes, he will guide you into all the truth" (Jn 16:13).

Those holding office in the Church are only in the service of the faith of the redeemed people of God: " 'I am a fellow servant with you and your brethren who hold the testimony of Jesus . . .' For the testimony of Jesus is the spirit of prophecy" (Rev 19:10). In Israel it was possible for the people of God as a whole to be unfaithful to God, because salvation had at this time still not been brought about definitively. But against the background of the eschatological accomplishment of salvation in Christ, it is, in the Catholic view, impossible for the redeemed people of God, the Church, to falter as the Church, since, if this were to happen, the eschatological character of accomplished salvation would be brought into desperate straits. In the perspective of this imperishable or unfailing quality of the "faith of the Church" ("the powers of death shall not prevail against it"), we may regard the charism of infallibility of the whole office in the Church as an implication of the eschatological, definitive salvation (reality, Word, and Scripture) for the time between the resurrection and the Parousia of the Lord. This eschatologically-based infallibility of the Church's faith is also parallel to the so-called *opus operatum* character of sacramental sanctification, of which the imperishable foundation of the Church as the primordial sacrament is the eschatological basis. Christ situated the fullness of the diaconate of sanctification in the Church, the fruit of his redemption. The imperishable quality of this diaconate, on a basis of the definitive accomplishment of salvation, is given concrete form in the unfaltering saving efficacity of the Church's sacraments for those who believe in Christ. The Word and the sacraments endure because of their eschatological foundation. What is called the "jurisdictional power" of the ecclesiastical office—really a "service"—only refers to the manner in which the Word and the sacraments are legitimately administered in the Catholic Church.

The infallibility of the "faith of the Church" (and all the mutually interacting elements implied in this, especially the infallibility of the Church's office in "matters of faith and morals") may therefore be traced back, not to a fixed possession of the Church on its own account, but to the power of Christ as the

Lord who holds the Church definitively in his hand. This infallibility is therefore a grace which visibly manifests itself in the Church.

The limits of the infallibility of the Church's authority will also be clear from this. This infallibility is a charism that preserves the whole desposit of faith throughout the entire life of the Church on earth until the Parousia. It is, however, no guarantee that the Church will experience all the aspects of the faith at their precise hierarchical value at all periods of its life. The imperishable existence of the Church, of which this infallibility is an implication, should not be regarded as something static. Whenever attention is directed in the Church to one particular detail in one definite period of the Church's existence rather than to the dynamic inviolability of the whole treasury of faith, the limits of this infallibility begin to reveal themselves. Although I cannot go into a detailed analysis of these limits here, I should like to indicate at least one of the functions of the Church's teaching authority: its function in the definition of dogma. This function is subordinate to the formal mission of the teaching office of the Church (Mt 28:18–20) to preserve and to hand down the testimony of the apostles in a pure, living form which will appeal to men at all times. The situation frequently necessitates a more precise definition, but here the apostolic tradition, the *paradosis*, acts as an objective norm to the Church's magisterium, and the carrying out of this function of defining dogma is subordinate to the Church's task of preserving the

93

apostolic testimony itself. The definition of dogma is never an isolated activity—dogma is not defined for the sake of the definition! There is, moreover, always a danger present in any definition of dogma, however necessary and beneficial it may be in certain situations, in that a precise definition of one aspect of faith may lead to the obscuring of another, complementary aspect. History provides evidence of the fact that one definition frequently requires another at a later period, the second definition integrating the "one-sidedness" of the first into a more perfect whole. Hilary, for example, alluded to the awkward situation into which the Church was often forced whenever it was obliged to define a datum of faith dogmatically in order to combat error.[16]

Conclusion

It will consequently be clear that I regard as alien to Catholicism both any exclusive assertion of the *sola scriptura*, the *sola traditio*, or the *solum magisterium*, and similarly any affirmation of two or three parallel and independent sources. Both the Scriptures and tradition are necessary to the life of the Church. But, on the other hand, Scripture and tradition also need the Church and each other if they are to be recognized as canonical scriptures and as authentically apostolic tradition. Apostolic Scripture is not Scripture as, for example, Marcion interpreted it, but as it is interpreted in the Church of Christ. The Church's supervision of scriptural exegesis does not place it above Scripture, but merely points to the Church's recognition of the exclusively apostolic principle as the norm of Christian faith and of life in the Church. And this recognition of the apostolic authority with regard to our faith means in the last resort to recognition of the *auctoritas*, the power and authority, of God as the only and the exclusive criterion of Catholic faith—the Father sent his Son and manifested himself in him, and Christ sent his apostles, who became the foundation of the Church.

4. Secular Worship and Church Liturgy

"The liturgy is the summit towards which the activity of the Church is directed; at the same time it is the fountain from which all the Church's power flows. . . . It inspires the faithful to become 'of one heart in Love' when they have tasted to the full of the paschal mysteries; it prays that 'they may grasp by deed what they hold by creed'."—*Constitution on the Sacred Liturgy*, I, 10.

D

Doubts about the meaning of Church liturgy

William Hamilton says: "I do not see how preaching, worship, prayer, ordination, the sacraments can be taken seriously by the radical theologian."[17] This radical movement of the Church towards the world has already turned its back on such theologians as Rudolf Bultmann (whom it regards as conservative) and the whole of the post-Bultmann school, and has even disposed of Harvey Cox, who makes such a furore in certain circles, with the pleasant insinuation of neo-orthodoxy—"The Secular City (pop Barth)." Even John A. T. Robinson, the author of *Honest to God*, is regarded as "behind the times". This movement is not an expression of something that has been thought out by scholars in their studies and found its way across the world by means of translations. In my opinion, the very opposite is nearer to the truth. What many believers have experienced in their own lives since 1945, whether they have liked it or not, has simply been formulated and expressed systematically by these "Christian atheists" or, as they prefer to call themselves, "radical theologians". The Episcopalian Paul van Buren has now said quite openly—and thus more candidly than in his book—not only that theist ideas have been finally discarded but that the living God of the Bible has simply ceased to count, and that he, a clergyman, has not prayed for a long time and avoids liturgical services. This is a frank expression of what I too have often heard in Catholic student circles, both clerical and lay, although I cannot really say how high the percentage is among Catholics. In any case, the phenomenon is a very real one. We must, of course, take a certain tendency to follow fashion partly into account, especially now that so many of such books (in which many readers recognize themselves) are available to all in cheap, easily accessible editions. But, however much this phenomenon may be influenced by fashion, our daily experiences prove beyond all doubt that "Christian atheism" is making giant strides throughout the world. Most young people, laymen and laywomen, who enrol as students in the theological faculty at a university have already read all the available books and articles in this field. The very fact that a surprisingly large number does enrol in such courses is proof of the intense interest in these intriguing aspects of the religious problem of life.

In such a climate, those who are engaged in renewing the liturgy are, of course, faced with serious problems. Liturgical worship itself is already becoming a basic problem for many people.[18] On the one hand, many older believers are shocked and upset by liturgical renewals, whereas many of the younger ones regard the entire liturgy, both in its

older and in its renewed form, as already out of date—
they have no further need for it. It is, of course, true
that this was said centuries ago, during the Enlighten-
ment, and the Church's liturgy has survived this
rejection for more than a century and a half, but
pointing out how relative such manifestations are in
the perspective of history will not make much
impression on those who support the new slogans.
Christians could react by saying, Very well, we will
write these people off as Christians and go over to
the Church's order of the day! I believe, however,
that it is not, in our present time, up to Christians
themselves to determine the moment when the
dialogue should be broken off. If it is broken off, then
this should be done from outside. The believer
himself should not take the initiative by threatening
anathema. At least, I do not think that anything
would be gained by it. But if the dialogue is broken
off from outside, then all that remains for a Christian
—averse to a ghetto Church, but certainly prepared
to regard a diaspora Church as a real possibility for
the future—is to bear witness, confess what Jesus,
the Christ (all he has left), means for him and
proclaim that the glorification of God's name *is*, *for
him*, still the deepest meaning of his human life. He
will, then, leave it to the future to judge who has
most profoundly and most purely approached the
relevance of human life and who has done most
justice to man.

None the less, Christians themselves, as believers
in God, must put their convictions into practice in

their own period, and for this reason they must listen to what H. Ringeling has called the "foreign prophecy" which appeals to us from the secularized world. Existential problems are rightly subjected to the criticism of Christianity, but in the same way Christian forms of life are subject to criticism in the light of new existential experiences. In the concrete, this latter criticism is directed towards a Christian life more or less identified with a "practice" of the faith in which liturgical worship runs parallel to a life which is fully immersed in the world. Any liturgical renewal which ignores this criticism will at the same time be ignoring the *kairos*, God's offer of grace here and now, and thus grace itself.

It is instructive to consider a passage taken from Paul Tillich's writings in connection with a text taken from one of the pronouncements made by the Second Vatican Council. In comparison with the new radical trend, both of these texts are "classical" theology and are therefore stigmatized as "out of date" by the radical theologians. The passage from Tillich is: "The existence of religion as a special realm is the most conspicuous proof of man's fallen state." The conciliar text is: "They err no less . . . who believe that they can plunge themselves into secular concerns, as though these had nothing to do with the religious life, because they think that religious life consists only of acts of worship and of fulfilling certain moral obligations. This discrepancy between the faith that they confess and their everyday life must be regarded as one of the more serious

errors of our times."[19] Both Tillich and the council
are saying that, from the Christian point of view, the
cleavage between worldly activity and liturgical worship is a disaster, and that this gap must be bridged.
But then we are faced with the question, how?
Should we regard secular life as worship and
separate worship as meaningless? Or should liturgical
worship be secularized and placed in the sphere of
secular life with its terrrestrial projects? Or does the
worship of God which is practised in and through
our worldly activity with our fellow-men of its very
nature still demand a grateful celebration in the
Church's liturgy? For, even if one denies that there
is a dilemma between service to mankind and the
glorifying of God's name—"God's glory is living
man" (Irenaeus)—this Christian commitment to
producing a world fit for all men to live in still
confronts us with the problem of whether this directly
useful service of our fellow-men does not call for the
glorifying of God's name in an act that is not directly
useful to the world—in other words, in the Church's
liturgy. Anthropologically speaking, the question is
this: Is *human life* meaningful without thanks-giving
celebrations? We may well ask ourselves, with
Gabriel Marcel, whether the disappearance of gratitude from the world is not a "falling off in wisdom".

It is therefore not a question of trying to find *some*
place in the world where man is failing constitutively
to give meaning to the world and thus, in spite of
everything, is still thrown back on God in order to
give himself meaning. The question is whether the

giving of thanks is not implicit in the ontological structure of our authentic being as men, and therefore whether our conquering intervention in the world in order to raise mankind (and here one could ask to what level?) is really the last word that can be said about man in the existential sense. Ethics are certainly necessary for the *human* cultivation of the world, but religion is not—even though religion is bound, via ethics, to give a distinctive complexion to this task and to give it the eschatological, definitive meaning which transcends, in grace, both all secularity and all ethics and which alone gives the world complete possession of itself.

Is religion unnecessary, then, to the secular plan, an "extra" whose meaning is to be found in itself, irrespective of its repercussions on the world? But, put in this way, is a religion which simply runs parallel to the created world still *real*?

All this presents us with a multitude of questions, but, to put it briefly, is Christianity concerned with God or with man? The radical theologians have passed final judgement on this already—it is concerned with man, and talking about God is simply an out-of-date Christian way of understanding man. Even Aquinas, who summarized simply the traditional Christian feeling in this matter, does not make it any easier for us. In his consideration of worship, prayer and the liturgy, he stated explicitly that worship is not necessary because of God, but because of man himself.[20] Not God, but religious man requires it, although in relation to God. But does man in a secularized world still require it? In any case, we still end up with the world again, in which man reaches his culminating point as a giver of meaning. The ultimate question, then, is whether man can really be called a completely secular being or whether the openness of his being as a person is not of such a nature that he cannot have his destiny within himself, not even in the "we" of relationship with another, since this too belongs within the sphere of the human person and has in its turn an unfathomable openness which cannot be filled by the secular.

Man, though he is not wholly "of the world" is in the world. That is why his religious practice cannot, on the one hand, be divorced from the reality of his secular activity; for our view of God would then not really be taking his being as God into account. God is, after all, the creator of this secular sphere, and he does not take back with his left hand what he has given to us with his right. A religion which is not at the same time secular, then, can hardly be called authentic—but, on the other hand, this does not determine what religion and worship *are*. Nevertheless we can readily take as our point of departure the statement that religion—Christianity—is a definite, qualified manner of being in the world.

Secular life as worship

St. Paul wrote to the Christians of Rome that they should present their lives "as a living sacrifice, holy and acceptable to God" and as "spiritual worship"

(Rom 12:1–2). Their "lives"—Paul said their "bodies" in the Semitic sense of all that belongs to man, the human person with all its secular implications. As a "body" man is with others in the world. This totality, the "world", as Paul said, is the place of "spiritual worship". In the Bible, among many other things, the "world" also means man in the world as God's good creation, deprived of glory by his sinfulness, but reborn in Christ as a "new creature" who is no longer doomed and who lives in a world liberated from the enslaving spirits of the world, of all kinds, both old and new. Christian life in the world, being concerned with the world and practising human solidarity, must therefore be, for the Christian, *worship* of God, glorifying God's name. Paul's admonition at the same time suggests that there is also a way of being active in the world that is not worship: there is Christian secularity and non-Christian secularity. Paul does not, however, imply that the Christian attitude deprives the secular of its integrity. It shares, still "groaning", in the "new creation", which is the Christian himself.

The Epistle to the Hebrews reveals the foundation of this early Christian view of worship even more clearly. Jesus did not give his life in a liturgical solemnity—on the contrary, in an obviously secular conflict, coloured though it was by religion, he remained faithful to God and to men and gave his life for his own in a secular combination of circumstances. Calvary was not a Church liturgy, but an hour of human life, which Jesus experienced as worship. In it, our redemption is to be found. We have not been redeemed by an act of pure worship, a liturgical service—our redemption was accomplished by an act which was part of Jesus' human life, situated in history and in the world. "For the one of whom these things are spoken [i.e. our Lord] belonged to another tribe, from which *no one has ever served at the altar*" (Heb 7:13). It is possible to speak of a secular liturgy, since the author of Hebrews applied to this self-sacrifice in the world the cultic categories of Jewish religion under the old law, thus endowing it with their sacred character. In this way the new concept of worship came into being—human life itself experienced as a liturgy or as worship of God. Cult thus acquired a new meaning in the New Testament—life in the world shared with one's fellow-men must itself be a "spiritual sacrifice". On the basis of Jesus' self-sacrifice, the Christian's life in this world can now become worship. In their life of faith in the world, the people of God are now wholly a "priestly people of God". All believers are now told "to be a holy priesthood, to offer spiritual sacrifices acceptable to God through Jesus Christ" (1 Pet 2:5). Faith itself is a "sacrificial offering (Phil 2:17) and every act of love of one's fellow-man is "a sacrifice acceptable and pleasing to God" (Phil 4:18). Doing good, mutual help and sharing with one another are now, in Christ, liturgy and worship (see Heb 13:16).

The New Testament clearly lays stress on "secular worship". Because the dawn of the eschatological life came with Christ—"And I saw no temple in the city, for its temple is the Lord God the Almighty and the Lamb" (Rev 21:22)—the profane or secular can become the pure expression of mankind's peace with God, as was fully apparent in the human life of Jesus.

That is why, for about three centuries, the first generations of Christians were proud of the fact that they had no churches or altars—one of the reasons why the pagans called them "atheists" or godless people. The pagan Celsus censured Christians: "Your eyes cannot bear temples, altars and images of God"[21]—for Christians, these were "idolatry". But the early Christians said this of themselves as well. Towards the end of the second century, Minucius Felix wrote: "We have no temples and no altars".[22] An absence of "religion" was the astonishing thing which particularly struck the pagans with regard to Christianity. This primitive Christian reaction against worship as something separate from ordinary life was related to the prophetic impulse in the Old Testament: "Do not trust in these deceptive words: 'This is the temple of the Lord, the temple of the Lord, the temple of the Lord'. . . . truly amend your ways and your doings, . . . truly execute justice one with another" (Jer 7:4–5). On the other hand, it is notable that as soon as Christians began to take over the external forms of pagan worship, the reproach of "atheism", as applied to them, disappeared from the writings of antiquity.

Christianity in its beginnings, owing to a one-sided eschatological orientation in which it was constantly anticipating the end of time, made no distinction between the secular and the "sacral". "Whether you eat or drink, or whatever you do, do all to the glory of God" (1 Cor 10:31). This *secular worship* was, so to speak, the novelty of the New Testament, in which a criticism of the old Jewish sacrifices and of the Old Testament distinction between profane and sacral, clean and unclean, is clearly discernible. The attention of the early Christians was directed less towards the Church than towards the kingdom of God, in which the whole of the created world was included. This eschatological Christianity saw the Christ not simply as the "head of the Church", but more universally as the one who had received dominion over the whole world. In Christ, Christians were no longer subjected to a world dominated by the powers of evil, but had themselves become the masters of the world—everything belonged to them, because they belonged to Christ (1 Cor 3:22–3). Redemption thus meant an exorcism, a de-deification and a de-demonization of the secular. Fate, the *moira* or *fatum* of the ancient world, had been overcome. This was the "new creation" that had been accomplished in Christ on the basis of his dying to and through the "old world". In Christ, *amen* could be said to the secular, which could now be experienced as worship, because, since Jesus, "all the fullness of God" had appeared on earth (Col 1:19).

Christian commitment to the ordering of human society here and now and Christian opposition to all injustice that disrupts peace among men—these may, then, rightly appeal to Scripture for their authority. In the situation in which Christianity finds itself in the world today, this commitment must be experienced as that secular worship required by the biblical essence of Christianity—secular life itself must be a "spiritual worship". Christian faith is not a flight *from* the world into the Church's liturgy. It aims to enable the world to share in the coming of the kingdom of God, a kingdom of peace, righteousness, and love. Faith affirms that human life in the world is ultimately meaningful and worth living, thanks to Jesus, the Christ. The Second Vatican Council repeatedly stated this Christian view—the eschatological expectation of Christianity does not limit the Christian task in this world, but rather completes it in the light of new motives. Christianity does not imply any neglect of the secular task, but, on the contrary, gives Christians a more intensive stimulus to carry it out. Their eschatological expectation urges Christians to work for a better world for all peoples.[23]

But then we are faced with this question: Does Christianity then merge into a more intensive commitment to one's fellow-man in the world, experienced as secular worship? Is Christianity intensified human solidarity? Or is it a song of praise, a *paneguris* (Heb 12:22) or a "festal gathering", in which the source of this greater fraternity which is experienced is praised in thanksgiving? Or, expressed in a different way: Is this intensified human solidarity, on the basis of the fact that God's revelation also gives man a deeper understanding of himself, conceivable and capable of being experienced without any explicit praise of God?

The liturgical worship of the Church

The integration of the profane and the sacral is therefore an *eschatological* reality. But the Christian is living in the interim, in the period of tension between the "already" and the "not yet"—Christ's kingdom is still developing in history. The Church is not yet the eschatological kingdom. This is still only on its way, and there is, precisely for this reason, still a factual difference between the "profane" or secular and the religious. The first Christian generations had to learn empirically that the *eschaton* had only just been set in motion. They had therefore to reinterpret earlier statements in the light of their later existential experiences. They underwent the painful experience of discovering that, although he who was in the Lord could not sin (1 Jn 3:9), Christians, like non-Christians, did in fact sin and die. There was still an element of sinfulness in their secular activity among men. Secularity in itself was not yet "secular liturgy". It was only secular liturgy by virtue of the Christian's faith in Jesus, the Christ, who made all things new.

Although the early Christians had no temples and altars, they did celebrate a Church liturgy in close connection with their "secular worship". Initially, these two were closely interwoven in the love-meal or *agape*, in which the secular liturgy of the community at table—"everything for the glory of God"—merged with the celebration of the Eucharist, so that it was difficult to say where the one liturgy ended and the other commenced. In any case, the reality of this secular worship, in its Christian dimension in depth, was explicitly celebrated in praising and thanking God and in preaching, instruction, and admonition; in other words, in a Church liturgy in which everything had to take place in accordance with the order of the Church.

Man's personal relationship with God can never occur in a "pure state", because it would then be an *empty* relationship without explicit content and religious man would be in danger of pursuing nothingness. Our love of God therefore always has—has indeed of its very nature—a basis in the world and in our fellow-men which brings it into the sphere of our experience. This does not, however, in any way imply that explicit and thematic religion, as brought to expression in silence with God (interior prayer) or in the ecclesial community of believers (the liturgy of the Word and the Sacrament), is the consequence of an outmoded "theist supernaturalism". Anyone who concludes, on the basis of the idea that man's living and personal relationship with God is of its nature rooted in and nourished by his relationship with his fellow-men in the world, that the Christian has *only* to devote himself consistently to the humanization of mankind by humanizing the world, without making any mention of God, is in my

opinion causing a short-circuit fatal to Christianity—
it could only be avoided by a consistent humanist
atheism. After all, anyone who states explicitly and
thematically that man's relationship with God is
implicitly contained in his relationship with the world
and his fellow-men has already reached the level of
an explicit profession of belief in God—for how,
otherwise, should he have any knowledge of this
implication? But then one must accept the consequences of this explicit knowledge if one is to
continue to be honest with oneself. As soon as one
becomes aware that the shared experience of community with God makes one's service to the world
and mankind a worship of God—in other words, as
soon as one accepts "secular worship" as Christian—
one must do justice to the fullness of this reality
(which is precisely a gift) and express this affirmation
in praise and thanksgiving. Anyone who really gives
and receives love in the day-to-day course of his life
is conscious at times of a need to express himself in a
gesture whose only significance is that it is a sign of
his love and gratitude.

In the final analysis, "not expressed" or "never
expressed" is the same thing as "irrelevant". But if
we insist that God is the *implicit* happiness of our
lives (and hence must remain implicit—that is, contained *in* our commitment to the world and our
fellow-men), we are saying something without really
wanting to express it. Humanist atheism seems to me
to be a more consistent attitude. Moreover, experience teaches that this position of exclusive

acknowledgement of God as the "transcendent third" in our human relationships cannot be maintained for very long—it soon turns either into explicit religion or the consistency of "atheism". In this respect, Paul van Buren's development is revealing. In a discussion about his book *The Secular Meaning of the Gospel*, he remarked frankly that he did not know what one gained or lost by calling a certain answer Christian or non-Christian. It seemed to him that one must say that around the figure of Christ Christianity has developed a fixed image of man and human relationships. So likewise has Western humanism. Whether and how far that humanism has been influenced by Christianity is a different question. If he were really pressed, he would probably say that he was more concerned with the content of that Christian image than with the name it was given, but if anyone wanted to make an issue of the name, he would have to admit that he was not quite a Christian. His position is thus the direct opposite of that of the Christian Rudolf Bultmann. This does not, of course, mean that van Buren may not possess the *reality* of Christianity experientially. But it is legitimate to ask whether a grateful awareness of the event from which we may really be living is not decisive for the reality of such a life. And it is precisely here that the significance of the Church and her liturgy come into focus.

Anyone accepting "secular *worship*" cannot escape the inner consequence of praise and thanksgiving. That many can accept the former—secular worship—and in all honesty not the latter—praise and thanksgiving—raises the question of whether this is not the result of a one-sided tendency in Western civilization which at least for the time being is blinding men to the possibilities of anything in life which differs from the things which appeal to Western man today. In this case faith must be critical of this civilization—or at least, of its particular bias—and at the same time it must consider afresh the consequences of this new experience, that is, of the manifestation of God apart from explicitly religious or ecclesial forms. For if man's experience of the "hidden God" comes increasingly into prominence in our times, the manifestation of God in the liturgical event will be increasingly obscured, unless the presence of God in the form of genuine human solidarity is experienced in a more real way than in the past. Anyone wishing to make a case for both a Church liturgy and secular worship will therefore have to take this new Christian experience into account, since the faithful community must be brought to the recognition of itself in the liturgy.

If then, praise and thanksgiving necessarily flow from the fact that the gift has in reality been given, and hence are evoked in an inward by by "secular worship", the relationship between the Church's liturgy and secular worship will reflect this. The *berākhāh*—the praise of God from which the Eucharist first took its structure—or the Church's present liturgy will, of course, be without value if the reality which sustains it, our relationship of service to our fellow men in the world, is not in fact there;

for this secular worship in its deepest dimension, as the gift of grace, is what is expressed and acknowledged in prayer and the liturgy within the intersubjective sphere of those who share the faith. Without secular worship, prayer, and the Church's liturgy, our speaking of and to God become simply an ideological suprastructure without roots in the realities of life, and hence artificial. Our praise of God's majesty and of his love for men—"God is my song"—belongs essentially to the total structure of our love of God which realizes itself in love and concern for our fellow-men.

The rhythm, frequency, and duration of this praise of God will naturally be determined by the prevailing social and historical conditions, and in sober and matter-of-fact times it will tend to be spread wider and thinner, although it is possible to argue that just such times are in greater need of warmth, splendour, and elegance in the liturgical sphere. The Eastern liturgies are charged, somewhat unfairly, with "estrangement from the world"; yet it is remarkably how secular worship and Church liturgy are harmoniously united in some of these liturgies, as when they explicitly invite the faithful, at the beginning of the eucharistic service, to reconcile themselves with their fellow men before joining in the sacrifice of praise. In the same way, Aquinas could say that "visiting widows and orphans" (the typically medieval form of social concern for one's fellow men, which could be translated into modern terms as help for the underdeveloped countries,

Christian protest against racial discrimination, and all forms of injustice) was itself worship, the glorifying of God's name, but that this precisely called for an explicit praise of God and Christian *eucharistia*. It is already clear in the case of Aquinas, who derived this view from the very heart of Christianity, that holiness and prayer are essentially identical with concern for one's fellow men in the world, and yet that precisely this secular kind of prayer and holiness needs to be expressed explicitly in praise and thanksgiving also. This is expressed as *anamnēsis* in the eucharistic prayer, in which God is praised and thanked for the miraculous deeds that he has wrought in our humanity and its history.[24]

Without secular worship, the Christian Eucharist itself becomes meaningless for us. On the other hand, however, the Eucharist is also the Church's *mission to* secular worship, which has been made possible because of the absolute self-sacrifice of Jesus' human life, suffering, and death. Secular worship and Church liturgy are not alternatives—they are two complementary, mutually evocative forms of the one Christianity. In St. John's gospel, the account of the washing of the disciples' feet occupies more or less the same place as the account of the Eucharist in the synoptics (the account that is "lacking" in John). Many exegetes have therefore maintained that the washing of the feet—service of one's fellow men— has a eucharistic significance. The Church's liturgy is a mission to secular worship, to real service of one's fellow men in the concretely existential situation of every individual and of the whole of mankind in the world situation of the twentieth century. The synoptics give an account of the *sacramentum*, whereas John gives an account of the *res sacramenti*, the reality that is signified and realized or to be realized—true fraternity with all men, in Christ. To make a division between the Eucharist and world history (as worship) is to misconceive the deepest meaning both of the Eucharist and of world history, since the latter may move towards and merge into the *eschaton*, thanks to the *ephapax*, the unique event of Jesus' humanity—he who was in absolute community with the living God and thus the Son of God in secular humanity. Through the Church's liturgy, believing man is brought "to the core of reality", *in* the world *with* God. The world itself is now involved in the doctrine of "justification" which was, in the past, conceived in too intimate and individualistic terms both by Catholic and by Protestant Christians. In this sense, American theology will undoubtedly inject fresh life into its older and often pretentious European counterpart.

This totality is strikingly expressed in the term which became firmly established during the council—the Church is the *sacramentum mundi*, the "sign of the world", the world itself brought to epiphany. The Church and her liturgy are the world, with its secular worship, at that profound level on which the world utters its own *mystery* in a conscious and mature confession; that mystery from which and in which it lives, thanks to Christ, and thus fulfils and realizes itself precisely as Christ's world; in which man too gives thanks for his Christian life in the world which moves freely towards the eternal kingdom of God. Hence we *celebrate* in the Church what is being accomplished outside our churches in human history, insofar as this can be called salvation history. In the Christian unity of secular worship and Church liturgy, *homo mundanus* coincides with *homo religiosus*.

In this way, I believe, both authentic aspects—the one being present in what is called "secularized" Christianity and the other in what is known as "conventional" Christianity—are rescued from the silt of inauthentic expressions and forms which may have covered them both.

Is Church liturgy then simply communal thanksgiving and homage? Yes, it is, but in such a way that reality is intensified and the accomplishment of man's mode of existence in the sign of Christ's resurrection is enhanced in it. The liturgy, after all, is carried out in the Church which believes that God's promise is fulfilled in Christ. In the liturgy of the Church, this promise is therefore accomplished in us, in me, because I enact, together with the Church, the faith of the Church and thus come, in faith, into contact with Jesus Christ, on whom the Church places its hope. It is in the Church's liturgy that God's grace in Christ is made publicly apparent—the promise is made true *now* in me, in the celebrating community. It is in this witness of faith that the *public* confession of the Christian conviction is made manifest—the *sacramentum fidei*, in other words, God's saving act in our sacramental, liturgical, visible activity of faith. God's grace thus manifests itself in our terrestrial history in a way that is most strikingly transparent to faith in the Church's liturgy, as an integrating part of the whole to which our "secular worship" also belongs, that other worship in which the same grace manifests itself in a different way and thus makes itself felt in a different way.

On closer consideration, the basic intention of the modern "desacralization" of the liturgy does not make it so strikingly different from the liturgy of the first ten centuries as might first appear. In both cases, it is the ordinary "concrete things" of human life which represent and realize the holy. In the "cosmocentric" view of man prevalent in the past, attention was directed towards physical things in the great world of creation, so that naturally water, oil, incense, icons and everything else that was materially visible were included as the expression of the Invisible. In the modern "anthropocentric" view of man, our attention is directed towards ethics—towards justice and love, and it is above all these realities of creation that are experienced as the manifestation of the Invisible.

In both cases, then, the point of departure is not an unjustified division between the world and the liturgy, but the insight in faith that the "new earth" is already being realized in a hidden manner. The believer who was orientated towards nature spoke above all of the "new earth". The present-day believer, on the other hand, prefers to speak of "new history", the "metropolis" and the "secular city" by virtue of the eschatological kingdom begun for us in Christ. The old exuberance of the "material signs" and thus of "nature" has given way to the new exuberance of human solidarity and thus of "history", but both express the *same* sacramental intention. Is this difference within the unity not a gain, a deepening, and a humanization rather than a loss? In itself, it is in any case not a weakening of the sacramental experience, but a translation of this experience into a different social context—less orientated towards "nature" and more orientated towards "history", less cosmic and more emphatically human—and in both cases it is the secular manifestation or sacrament of grace.

Not only the physical but everything else which belongs to humanity is experienced as the sacramental manifestation of God's presence. It is precisely for this reason that the celebration of the community is once again stressed in the liturgy and that the communication of the divine is conceived *less* in material categories than in the "real presence" of Christ in his assembled people, who demand justice and love for all men. It is precisely for this reason that the present-day believer can no longer experience the real presence in the Eucharist "considered in isolation"—that is, experienced separately from Christ's real presence in the assembled congregation. It is not a question of denying one concept in favour of the other but of making the material world of *man in community* central, with the result that the *whole* becomes the sacrament of God's manifestation in Christ. The fact that the whole human person and his physical mode of existence are committed at the same time—a commitment in which the man Jesus has gone before us—prevents the liturgy from being one-sidedly either materialized or spiritualized. Human solidarity has therefore acquired its own sacramental form in the renewed liturgy, so that the breach between life and liturgy, a consequence of the change in the West from "cosmocentric" to "anthropocentric" thinking, in which the liturgy lagged behind, can once again be healed. Worship and life thus join hands more cordially and the Church's liturgy is again becoming the *sacramentum mundi*, or rather, the sacrament of the *historia mundi*, of the world of men which, in the sign of Jesus' resurrection, moves towards the eschatological kingdom in which terrestrial history is, by God's power, perpetuated in eternity.

All this will have inescapable consequences for the further renewal of the liturgy, both in its content and in its structure. The liturgical cult will not be able to ignore the total structure of secular worship and its epiphany in the Church's liturgy. A liturgy which spoke only of the hereafter and ignored the concrete history of the world, which is precisely the place where the *eschaton* is mysteriously in the process of becoming, would be a liturgy which forgot the Johannine account of the washing of the disciples' feet, a *liturgia gloriae* which left out the period and the realm in which people are engaged with all their heart and soul. How could life and liturgy then form a unity, as the council asked, without making a division between the secular and the religious? If this division is not avoided, the Church's liturgy will not survive; it will become estranged from the world— and then Christians will, of course, abandon it.

If, on the other hand, the Church's liturgy were reduced to what presupposes and at the same time gives rise to liturgy—that is, "secular worship", in which God is only implicitly experienced in secular life, or brought down to the level of a pleasant little chat consisting of "good morning" and "have a nice week-end"—then this liturgy would be a serious misconception not only of the "spiritual sacrifice" implied by man's being in the world in the light of community with God but also of the profoundly human dimension which is expressed in the thankful celebration of all that gives our lives meaning and makes them worth living. And this is certainly no trivial commonplace, but the "seriousness of divine love", made historically tangible among us in Jesus' human love of God which had the form of a radical love of men "to the end".

As long as God is not "all in all", there is, it is true, no division between the Christian's life in the Church and his life in the world, but there is certainly an inner tension between them. The profane is not a category of the kingdom of God, because it is in the profane that the kingdom of God will completely penetrate the whole of creation and thus give it its highest autonomous freedom and its transparency to the divine. The profane is a provisional category—a category of the *coming* of the kingdom of God; of this kingdom's state of becoming. As long as this time of becoming lasts, so too will the duality of secular and Church worship remain valid and in force for the Christian. No practice of religion is possible which does not at the same time draw everyone and everything into its orbit, but without doing away with the secularity of the world. Secular activity is a part of the eucharistic sacrifice. Indeed, as for Jesus himself, so for the Christian, the "spiritual sacrifice" of everyday life in the world with one's fellow men is *the* sacrifice that matters; it is in this life in the world that the Christian finds the *reality* of his living participation in the sacrifice of Christ, the sacramental form of which he may receive as nourishment in the Eucharist, as his confession in faith that secular worship is only possible by virtue of God's "new creation" in Christ. Thus the fact that the worship proper to human history in this world has become possible thanks to Jesus' absolute love of men, which was itself the worship of God, is presented to the whole world as a sign in the Church's liturgy. History is to be brought to a good end in Christ. This is the indestructible Christian hope which impels us not only to improve the world and militantly to resist everything that may make the history of salvation a history that is opposed to salvation, but also to praise and thank God in the Eucharist, a praise that will ultimately sound like the *berākhāh* which, according to John, Jesus pronounced on the eve of his death: "I glorified thee on earth, *by completing the work* which thou gavest me *to do*" (Jn 17:4). Glorifying God's name is building the world of men, by the power of Jesus, the Christ, into a "communion of saints", a kingdom of peace, justice, and love, and at the same time "recollecting" that all this is an unmerited gift that is as characteristic of God—as "natural" to him—as is his entire being. This unquestioning divine goodness continues to be, for problematic human life, a problem which both attracts and repels and which is in any case unfathomable. The only adequate answer to it is unconditional surrender.

NOTES

1. F. J. J. Buytendijk, "Zur Phänomenologie der Begegnung", *Eranos-Jahrbuch* XIX (1950), 468.

2. *De carnis resurrectione*, 8 (*PL* 2, 806).

3. Augustine, *Ep.* 187, 34 (*PL*, 38, 845).

4. Leo the Great, *Sermo* 74, 2 (*PL* 54, 398).

5. Augustine, *In Ev. Joh.* 9, 10 (*PL* 35, 1463).

6. Denzinger-Schönmetzer 3857 (= Denzinger-Bannwart 2301).

7. DS 3806.

8. Aquinas, *Summa Theologiae*, III, q. 39, a. 5; and II–II, q. 1, a. 9, ad 3m.

9. *Summa Theologiae*, III, q. 49, a. 3, ad 1m.

10. Ambrose, *Apologia prophetae David* XII, 58 (*PL* 14, 916).

11. Another image with earlier origins than that of marriage can be found in Deuteronomy, which—unlike Hosea—conceived the mutual love between God and his people, not as an analogy of married love, but as an analogy of secular, political friendly relations between the king and his people. This relationship was dependent on a covenant love, and was expressed in affectionate obedience and loyal service to the king.

12. See E. Schillebeeckx, *Christ the Sacrament of Encounter with God*, London and New York, Sheed & Ward, 1963, chap. 3, sec. 1/3.

13. H. Renckens, *The Religion of Israel*, London and New York, Sheed & Ward, 1967, 40.

14. See, for example, C. H. Dodd, *The Old Testament in the New*, London, 1952.

15. Ignatius, *Ad Philad.* 4, 1; and Augustine, *De doctrina christiana* II, 14 (*PL* 34, 42).

16. *De trinitate* II, 2 (*PL* 10. 51).

17. T. Altizer and W. Hamilton, *Radical Theology and the Death of God*, New York 1966, 7.

18. See P. L. Berger, *The Noise of Solemn Assemblies*, New York 1961.

19. Paul Tillich, *Theology of Culture*, New York and Oxford 1964, 42; and *Pastoral Constitution on the Church in the Modern World*, I, 4, 43.

20. *Summa Theologiae* II–II, q. 91, a. 1, ad 3; q. 89, a. 1, ad 2; q. 81, a. 1, ad 1; etc.

21. Origen, *Contra Celsum* VII, 62 and 63–4.

22. *Octavius* 32, 1 (*CSEL* II, 45).

23. *Pastoral Constitution on the Church in the Modern World* I, 21, 39, and 43.

24. *Summa Theologiae* II–II, q. 81, a. 1, ad 1; a. 3; a. 4, ad 2; a. 8; q. 91, a. 1, ad 1 and ad 2; etc.